AI for Beginners Made Easy

Master AI Faster Than Ever with Easy Steps and
Proven Techniques to Explode Your Career in a
Blink of an Eye

Jamie K. Avery

TABLE OF CONTENTS

INTRODUCTION

In the ever-evolving landscape of technology, understanding artificial intelligence (AI) has become not just an advantage but a necessity. Regardless of your background—whether you're a newcomer to tech, a seasoned professional seeking to bolster your capabilities, an educator eager to update curricula, or a student aiming to enhance your academic repertoire—grasping the fundamentals of AI will open doors to incredible opportunities. Consider the transformative influence AI exerts on diverse sectors: from revolutionizing healthcare through advanced diagnostics to reshaping transportation with autonomous vehicles, AI's applications have reached unprecedented heights, embedding itself in our daily routines and profoundly altering the world around us.

Imagine navigating a city without a map; this is akin to ignoring AI developments. To truly harness the wealth of possibilities around you, a foundational understanding of AI is indispensable. This book serves as your map, guiding you through AI's intricate terrain with clarity and precision. It is crafted for readers with varied experiences and objectives but shares one common goal: to provide comprehensive insights into AI, empowering you to incorporate its principles into your personal and professional lives.

Throughout these pages, you'll embark on a journey designed as a friendly tour of AI's concepts, tools, and applications. From the basics to more complex ideas, this book lays out a structured pathway for learning, ensuring that by the time you reach the final chapter, you will not only have grasped AI's core tenets but also feel confident in applying them practically. You'll find each chapter building upon the last, creating a seamless flow that transforms seemingly daunting information into manageable, digestible parts.

Interactive elements play a crucial role in making this book a dynamic learning experience. As you progress, you'll engage with hands-on exercises and real-world applications that bring theoretical knowledge to life. Picture yourself developing a chatbot, capable of interacting with users in meaningful ways, or analyzing business data to unearth trends that could drive strategic decisions. Within a week, you'll be equipped with the skills necessary to bring such innovations to fruition, transforming mere curiosity into tangible expertise.

Moreover, this book fosters an enthusiasm for ongoing engagement with AI material. It's not just about acquiring knowledge but envisioning how this newfound understanding can propel you toward your own successes. Whether it's streamlining workflows, enhancing classroom instruction, or elevating project outcomes, each reader's journey will culminate in unique achievements made possible through AI.

As you dive into this exploration of artificial intelligence, embrace a mindset focused on growth and continuous learning. Think of this book as your guide to uncovering a fascinating new world, much like adopting a hobby where every discovery leads to deeper insight. Similar to how a gardener patiently tends to plants and learns nature's rhythms, you too will cultivate a rich understanding of AI's nuances as you delve deeper into its study. Approach each topic with an open mind and a sense of wonder at what lies ahead.

Curiosity is your most powerful tool throughout this endeavor. The field of AI is expansive, with new advancements and breakthroughs occurring regularly. By nurturing a desire to explore, challenge assumptions, and build upon foundational knowledge, you'll unlock creative potential and master AI applications beyond the confines of this text. The skills you'll acquire are not static; they will evolve alongside technological progress, becoming assets that stay relevant and adaptable across various fields.

From beginners taking their first steps into technology and professionals striving to remain competitive, to educators aiming to enrich their teaching practices and students preparing to enter the STEM workforce, this book addresses each audience's unique needs while fostering a shared pursuit of mastery over AI. Welcome this opportunity to enhance your abilities, broaden your horizons, and contribute meaningfully to a future increasingly defined by artificial intelligence.

With this introduction, you're poised to begin an exciting and informative expedition into the heart of AI. Prepare yourself to uncover the profound yet accessible world where technology and creativity converge, shaping tomorrow in remarkable ways. Let your adventure begin!

CHAPTER 1

Understanding Artificial Intelligence

U nderstanding artificial intelligence is crucial for navigating the modern technological landscape. AI is rapidly changing the way we interact with technology, from smart assistants that understand our speech to algorithms that predict our needs and behaviors. Whether in healthcare, finance, or social media, AI applications are evident in countless aspects of everyday life. The potential of AI seems limitless: machines learn new tasks, assist in complex decision-making, and even collaborate creatively. As we stand on the brink of this technological frontier, it's essential to have a firm grasp on what AI entails, its fundamental components, and its implications for the future.

In this chapter, readers will explore the fundamentals of artificial intelligence, beginning with its definition and historical roots. Key milestones in AI development, such as the creation of neural networks, will be highlighted to show how these systems mimic human learning processes. The text will also delve into the core components of AI systems—data, algorithms, and computing power—and their roles in enabling machine intelligence. By understanding these elements, readers will gain insights into how AI functions and the diverse ways it is applied across industries. Additionally, the distinction between narrow and generalized AI will be explained, illustrating the differences in capability and application. Finally, the chapter will discuss AI's integration into daily life, examining the benefits and challenges presented by this advancing technology. Through a detailed exploration of these topics, the chapter aims to equip readers—from novices to seasoned professionals—with a comprehensive foundation for understanding AI's scope and significance.

Definition and History of Artificial Intelligence

Artificial Intelligence (AI) marks a fascinating frontier in technology, embodying the simulation of human-like intelligence within machines and computer systems. By attempting to mirror cognitive functions such as learning and problem-solving, AI strives to create systems capable of reasoning, adapting to new information, recognizing patterns, understanding natural language, and even perceiving emotions under certain constraints. At its core, AI enables machines to perform tasks that typically require human intelligence, thus opening up diverse applications across numerous fields.

The historical roots of AI trace back to seminal figures such as Alan Turing, often considered one of the founding parents of modern computing and artificial intelligence. Turing's contributions laid the groundwork for how we conceptualize machine intelligence today. His pioneering work in the 1930s and 1940s, particularly the development of the Turing Machine, posed critical questions about the nature of computation and the potential for machines to exhibit intelligent behavior. This early inquiry into whether machines can think heralded the initial steps in the evolution of AI technologies, setting a theoretical bedrock for future advancements.

As AI progressed from theory towards practical solutions, pivotal milestones marked its transformative journey. One of these significant developments is the creation of neural networks, which mimic the structure and functioning of the human brain. Neural networks have revolutionized AI by enabling machines to learn from data inputs rather than being explicitly programmed for specific tasks. This breakthrough has facilitated advancements in areas like image recognition, speech processing, and decision-making systems, wherein algorithms can continuously improve through exposure to large datasets. The shift from early rule-based systems to adaptive learning models exemplifies AI's transition from theoretical concepts to tangible technological innovations.

Today, AI's integration into various sectors demonstrates its dynamic growth and evolving capabilities. In healthcare, AI assists in diagnosing diseases more accurately by analyzing complex medical data. In finance, AI algorithms help in detecting fraudulent activities and managing investments with greater precision. Meanwhile, in transportation, autonomous vehicles leverage AI technologies for navigation and obstacle avoidance, highlighting a move towards safer and more efficient travel experiences. Even mundane aspects of daily life, like voice assistants and recommendation systems, showcase AI's role in enhancing convenience and personalization.

This ongoing development underscores AI's immense potential, yet it also reflects the rapid pace at which this technology continues to evolve. As an ever-expanding field, AI raises intriguing questions about the future of human-machine interaction and the ethical considerations inherent in developing increasingly autonomous systems. The continuous refinement of AI applications not only emphasizes its present-day significance but also invites speculation on its future trajectory—how these intelligent systems might transform industries, impact job markets, and redefine societal norms.

Core Components of AI Systems

Artificial Intelligence (AI) systems are complex and multifaceted, composed of several essential components. Understanding these components is crucial for anyone looking to learn about AI, from beginners to professionals seeking to enhance their skills.

Data is the lifeblood of AI systems; it's the key element in AI learning and hugely impacts system performance and effectiveness. Without data, AI systems cannot function or improve. Consider how AI is used in predicting weather patterns: vast amounts of historical weather data are fed into the system. The quality and quantity of this data can directly affect the accuracy of the system's predictions. Thus, handling data responsibly—ensuring it's clean, relevant, and sufficient—is foundational for any successful AI application. A guideline to remember is that more meaningful data often leads to better AI outcomes.

Next, we delve into algorithms, the true backbone of AI decision-making. Algorithms are sophisticated sets of instructions that enable computers to process data and produce meaningful outputs. For example, facial recognition software relies on algorithms to match captured images with stored data to identify individuals. Just as a recipe guides a cook to create a dish, algorithms guide AI systems to derive insights and make decisions. Each algorithm is tailored to address specific problems, transforming raw data inputs into actionable information. When working with AI, one must appreciate the diversity of algorithms available and their applications.

In conjunction with data and algorithms, computing power plays a critical role in an AI system's operational efficiency. It determines how quickly and effectively a system can process complex computations. Modern AI applications often require immense processing capabilities, necessitating the use of advanced hardware such as GPUs and TPUs. This power enables operations like training deep learning models, which can involve millions of parameters. In fields such as autonomous driving, where real-time data processing is a must, robust computing power ensures that systems can make split-second decisions accurately and safely. Therefore, investing in adequate computing infrastructure is vital for scaling AI solutions.

Lastly, human interaction significantly influences AI ethics and usability. As AI becomes increasingly integrated into everyday life, it's important to consider how humans interact with these technologies. The ethical dimensions of AI encompass issues like privacy, bias, and accountability. To illustrate, consider AI systems used in hiring processes. If the data used to train these systems reflects societal biases, it could lead to unfair hiring decisions. Hence, developing AI responsibly includes actively monitoring and mitigating biases. Educators, developers, and policymakers must collaborate to ensure AI technologies advance in ways beneficial to society at large.

Human interaction also affects the usability of AI systems. Building user-friendly interfaces and ensuring transparency in AI decision-making helps users understand and trust the technology. Systems designed with end-users in mind enhance overall adoption and efficacy. For instance, virtual assistants like Siri or Alexa are successful because they are easy to use and seamlessly integrate into daily routines. Their intuitive design encourages user engagement, showing how critical user-centered design is to AI success.

The Difference Between Narrow and Generalized AI

In the realm of artificial intelligence (AI), understanding the distinction between narrow AI and generalized AI is fundamental. These two categories represent different capabilities and potential applications for AI technologies. Let's delve into what sets them apart and why their differences matter for the future of AI development.

Narrow AI, sometimes referred to as weak AI, is designed to perform a specific task or a set of tasks within a defined domain. It operates under a more restricted scope compared to its generalized counterpart. A prime example of narrow AI is the technology powering voice assistants like Siri or Alexa. These systems excel at understanding speech, answering questions, setting reminders, and playing music upon request. Their functionality, however, is confined to the tasks they were programmed to handle. They cannot learn or comprehend tasks outside of their designed purpose, such as cooking a meal or diagnosing a health condition independently.

The efficiency of narrow AI stems from its ability to focus on a particular problem without the need to process unrelated information. This specialization allows narrow AI to surpass human performance in specific areas, such as chess-playing algorithms that consistently defeat grandmasters. In industries like healthcare, narrow AI tools are employed for tasks like analyzing medical images or predicting patient outcomes based on data patterns. The precision of these specialized systems enhances productivity and fosters innovation by automating routine processes and freeing up human professionals to engage in more complex decision-making tasks.

In contrast, generalized AI represents the aspirational side of artificial intelligence. Also known as strong AI or artificial general intelligence (AGI), this concept envisions machines with the ability to understand, learn, and apply knowledge across a wide range of domains, much like a human can. Generalized AI would be capable of performing any intellectual task that a human being can undertake, including abstract reasoning, problem-solving in varied contexts, and even possessing self-awareness.

Despite significant strides in AI research, generalized AI remains a theoretical goal rather than a practical reality. Creating an AI system with human-like cognitive abilities poses immense challenges, both technical and ethical. The complexity of replicating the nuanced decision-making processes humans use daily is not yet achievable with current technology. However, the pursuit of AGI continues to drive research efforts, with the hope that one day, machines may fully emulate human cognitive functions.

Grasping the discrepancy between narrow AI and generalized AI is crucial for anticipating future advancements in AI research. Understanding these distinctions allows us to appreciate where we stand today and what innovations might lie ahead. For instance, while narrow AI is prevalent in many aspects of our daily lives, the advent of generalized AI could revolutionize how we interact with technology, potentially transforming various sectors like education, healthcare, and transportation.

As narrow AI makes its mark across different industries, its real-world impacts spark debates about productivity and employment. On one hand, narrow AI significantly boosts efficiency, automating tedious tasks and allowing businesses to operate more effectively. On the other hand, this automation raises questions about job displacement and the shifting landscape of employment. As AI technologies continue to evolve, some jobs may become obsolete, necessitating a workforce transition towards roles that require advanced skills beyond what narrow AI can provide.

The integration of narrow AI into workplaces encourages a reassessment of skill requirements and educational priorities. Workers may need to adapt by acquiring new competencies, particularly those focusing on creativity, critical thinking, and emotional intelligence — attributes that AI struggles to replicate. As organizations embrace AI-driven solutions, the collaboration between humans and machines becomes essential, harnessing the strengths of both to achieve optimal results.

To navigate these changes, stakeholders should consider strategic approaches to workforce development and policy formulation. Emphasizing education in STEM fields, promoting lifelong learning opportunities, and creating safety nets for displaced workers are vital measures to ensure that society reaps the benefits of narrow AI without leaving anyone behind. Additionally, cultivating a culture of innovation will empower individuals to harness AI technologies creatively, opening pathways to new career possibilities and economic growth.

How AI Fits into Our Daily Lives

Artificial intelligence has become deeply embedded in our daily lives, often in ways that are seamless and intuitive. One of the most prevalent uses of AI is in the tools and applications we interact with day in and day out, particularly on social media platforms. Social media algorithms are powered by AI to analyze user behavior and preferences, constantly learning to make each user's experience more personalized. For instance, when you see content tailored to your interests or ads that seem to predict your needs, that's AI at work. These algorithms aim to increase engagement by showing users posts and advertisements likely to spark interest, thus keeping them on the platform longer. The power of AI in these tools lies in its ability to process vast amounts of data rapidly, providing insights that would be impossible for humans to discern quickly.

Moving beyond social media, AI plays a crucial role in optimizing routine activities, particularly within smart home devices. Consider how smart thermostats adjust heating or cooling based on usage patterns and habits, aiming to create an optimal living environment while conserving energy. Similarly, AI-integrated smart speakers can manage tasks from setting reminders to playing music, all controlled by voice commands. These devices learn from user interactions to enhance their responses and efficiency, simplifying everyday tasks and increasing convenience. As homes become more connected, the influence of AI grows, embedding itself into daily routines in ways that enhance life quality without requiring much user intervention.

The entertainment industry also showcases AI's transformative potential, especially through personalized content recommendations. Streaming services like Netflix and Spotify utilize AI algorithms to suggest shows, movies, and music based on past viewing or listening behavior. By analyzing what users watch or listen to, AI makes educated guesses about new content they might enjoy, creating a unique entertainment experience tailored to individual tastes. This personalization does not just improve user satisfaction; it helps content providers retain subscribers and expand their audience by continually refining the accuracy of recommendations. Through AI, the entertainment landscape evolves, offering a library that feels curated to personal preferences.

Beyond just enhancing individual experiences, AI integration holds broader social and economic implications, particularly concerning job markets. The efficiencies introduced by AI have begun reshaping various industries, leading to discussions about the future of work and employment. Automation driven by AI can perform repetitive tasks more efficiently than humans, which significantly impacts manufacturing and service sectors. While this may lead to reduced demand for certain roles, it simultaneously creates opportunities for new kinds of jobs centered around AI technology development, management, and maintenance. Thus, there is a growing need for workers to adapt by gaining new skills pertinent to working alongside AI systems. This shift prompts educational reforms to prepare individuals for the evolving job market, emphasizing the importance of digital literacy and continuous learning.

Current State and Future Perspectives of AI

The present-day landscape of artificial intelligence (AI) is a dynamic panorama, marked by continuous advancements that extend across various sectors such as healthcare, finance, transportation, and entertainment. In healthcare, AI algorithms have transformed patient diagnostics and personalized medicine, enhancing the accuracy and efficiency of treatments. Financial institutions utilize AI for pattern recognition in fraud detection, providing more secure transactions. The integration of AI in transportation, notably through autonomous vehicles, revolutionizes how we perceive mobility and logistics, offering safer and more efficient travel options. Additionally, AI's role in entertainment through content recommendations has reshaped user experiences, tailoring offerings to individual preferences.

Tracking current trends within the AI ecosystem offers valuable insight into strategically integrating these technologies into personal and professional environments. For individuals, understanding AI applications can lead to more informed decisions about career opportunities and skill development in tech-driven markets. Professionals harness AI to automate routine tasks, optimize workflow efficiencies, and drive data-driven decision-making processes. For businesses, keeping abreast of AI developments helps maintain a competitive edge, allowing for innovative solutions that meet evolving consumer demands. Regularly monitoring these trends ensures that stakeholders remain adaptable and prepared to embrace AI's potential.

As we peer into the future of AI, speculations abound concerning its capabilities and impact. Concepts like advanced machine learning, natural language processing, and neural networks promise to push the boundaries of what AI can achieve. Imagining a world where machines exhibit genuine creativity or solve complex global challenges inspires both excitement and caution. These projections, though speculative, serve as catalysts for innovation, encouraging researchers and developers to explore uncharted territories in technology. This anticipation stirs curiosity among enthusiasts and skeptics alike, prompting dialogue on ethical considerations, regulatory frameworks, and the balance between human and machine collaboration.

Recognizing ongoing research efforts underscores the continuously evolving nature of AI and its broader societal implications. Academic institutions, tech companies, and independent labs worldwide are in relentless pursuit of breakthroughs that redefine AI's capacities. Research in areas like quantum computing aims to overcome existing limitations in processing power, potentially accelerating AI's ability to handle intricate computations. Meanwhile, explorations in ethics and transparency seek to ensure that AI systems are developed responsibly, with fairness and accountability at their core. By highlighting these endeavors, we appreciate not only AI's current progression but also its transformative potential for future generations.

The widespread adoption and influence of AI are indicative of a technological shift that permeates everyday life. As AI applications become more prolific, they reshape industries and redefine how services are delivered and consumed. This transformation prompts educational institutions to integrate AI literacy into curricula, preparing students to navigate and contribute to this digital evolution. Simultaneously, policy-makers must engage with AI advancements to enact regulations that foster innovation while safeguarding public interests.

CHAPTER 2

Exploring Machine Learning

Exploring machine learning involves an insightful journey through its diverse methods and applications. At its core, machine learning empowers computers to analyze data patterns and make informed decisions without explicit programming for every task. This chapter will provide an in-depth look at the foundational elements of machine learning, shining a light on how it transforms raw data into valuable insights. Understanding the fundamental differences between various types of machine learning is crucial for anyone wishing to harness the true potential of this technology. Whether you're a beginner taking your first steps or a seasoned professional seeking to deepen your knowledge, grasping these concepts will equip you with the tools needed to maximize the effectiveness of machine learning models in real-world scenarios.

In the pages ahead, readers will delve into the distinctions between supervised and unsupervised learning, each offering unique techniques and strategies for processing data. Supervised learning relies on labeled datasets to predict outcomes based on historical patterns, making it ideal for situations where specific results are desired. Conversely, unsupervised learning searches for hidden patterns within unlabeled data, offering innovative perspectives when predefined labels are unavailable. Moreover, the chapter touches upon common algorithms used in both learning approaches, enabling a comprehensive understanding of their implementation and benefits. Through this exploration, we'll also uncover the vital role data plays in model training and address challenges involved in evaluating and selecting the most suitable method for different projects. By navigating these topics, readers will be well-prepared to apply machine learning methodologies effectively, regardless of their field or objective.

Supervised vs. Unsupervised Learning

Machine learning is an exciting field that has revolutionized the way we solve complex problems by allowing computers to learn from data. This learning can be categorized primarily into two types: supervised and unsupervised learning. Understanding these categories is crucial for anyone venturing into machine learning, as each method offers unique tools and approaches to data interpretation and decision-making.

Supervised learning is like teaching a child with examples. Imagine you have a vast collection of images, some labeled with the word "cat" and others with the word "dog." A supervised learning model uses this labeled data to learn the difference between the two animals. By identifying features such as fur color, ear shape, and tail length, the model predicts which label fits new, unseen images. In essence, it learns a mapping from input features to output labels. This type of learning is widely used in applications where we need precise predictions based on historical data, such as predicting stock prices, diagnosing diseases, or even recognizing spoken words.

The process begins with gathering datasets that are well-labeled. These datasets act as mentors, guiding the algorithm in understanding the relationships within the data. Algorithms such as linear regression, decision trees, and neural networks are common tools employed here, each offering different strategies for drawing connections between inputs and expected outputs.

On the flip side, unsupervised learning operates without such explicit guidance. Here, the task involves exploring data without predefined labels. It's akin to discovering patterns and structures hidden within information just waiting to be unraveled. For instance, if given a collection of news articles, an unsupervised learning algorithm might cluster them into topics without knowing beforehand what those topics should be. This form of learning is particularly beneficial when we lack labeled datasets but still want to draw insights or detect anomalies.

Clustering is a primary mechanism in unsupervised learning, where data points are grouped based on similarities. Popular algorithms include k-means clustering and hierarchical clustering. These approaches help identify inherent groupings within data, which can later be pivotal in personalizing content or detecting fraud.

To choose appropriately between these two methods, one must consider each method's strengths and weaknesses. Supervised learning shines when specific outcomes are defined and abundant labeled data exists. However, it struggles with unseen scenarios where the data may not closely resemble historical patterns. Unsupervised learning, while excellent for discovering hidden structures in data without preconceived notions, often faces challenges in interpretability and requires careful evaluation to ensure meaningful results.

The decision framework to select the right learning method is heavily influenced by the nature of the problem at hand. Start by analyzing the available data: Is it labeled, or does it require discovery? Consider the goal: Are you aiming for precise predictions or innovative insights? For supervised learning, it's crucial to have a substantial amount of labeled data to effectively train the model. Known applications such as automated diagnosis in healthcare depend on vast amounts of patient data with accurate labeling to guide the AI in making reliable predictions.

Conversely, unsupervised learning is more flexible when it comes to data requirements and can be employed to make sense of data where labels are missing or impractical to obtain. Market segmentation in business analysis frequently leverages this advantage, where companies attempt to uncover customer segments and tailor their marketing strategies accordingly.

Moreover, the choice isn't always binary; sometimes, a combination of both methods, known as semi-supervised learning, can be advantageous. This approach takes the few labeled data points to guide training while simultaneously exploring the unlabeled dataset, thereby optimizing resources and improving model robustness.

By mastering the principles of supervised and unsupervised learning, readers can enhance their ability to make informed choices about which method best suits their projects. As they dive deeper into machine learning, understanding the nuances of each category equips them to tackle challenges with confidence, ensuring that they deploy the right algorithms to extract actionable insights from their data.

Basic Algorithms in Machine Learning

In the expansive world of machine learning, understanding key algorithms is crucial for grasping its application across various fields. These algorithms serve as the backbone of many technological advancements, shaping how machines learn from data to make predictions or decisions without being explicitly programmed.

To begin, linear regression stands out as a foundational algorithm that is instrumental in predicting continuous outcomes. It operates on the principle of modeling the relationship between a dependent variable and one or more independent variables by fitting a linear equation to observed data. This simplicity makes it an excellent starting point for beginners venturing into machine learning. For example, businesses might use linear regression to forecast sales or determine trends over time based on historical data. By examining past relationships between variables, linear regression helps to predict future outcomes, providing valuable insights for decision-making processes. Its straightforward nature allows for immediate application, offering solid ground for exploring more complex algorithms down the line.

Following linear regression, we encounter decision trees—another pivotal algorithm that simplifies complex classification and regression tasks. Decision trees work by splitting data into subsets based on feature value tests, constructing a tree-like model of decisions. This intuitive approach mirrors human decision-making processes, making it accessible for those new to the field. Whether determining customer churn in telecom industries or diagnosing diseases in healthcare, decision trees provide a visual and interpretable method to classify data. Their strength lies in their ability to handle both categorical and numerical data seamlessly, often requiring less data preprocessing compared to other algorithms. Additionally, decision trees can be pruned to avoid overfitting, ensuring that the model remains relevant and accurate as it grows in complexity.

Next, support vector machines (SVM) step in with their unique capacity to classify data using optimal hyperplanes. Unlike previous methods, SVM focuses on finding the hyperplane that best separates classes within a dataset. This is particularly useful when dealing with high-dimensional spaces or datasets with clear margins of separation. Take, for instance, image classification tasks where SVM excels in distinguishing patterns within pixels, aiding in facial recognition systems or handwriting analysis. The power of SVM lies in its ability to transform input data into higher dimensions, leveraging kernel tricks to solve nonlinear problems. Although it can be computationally intensive, the precision and scalability of SVM make it a preferred choice for many professionals aiming to refine their analytical skills.

Finally, the K-Nearest Neighbors (KNN) algorithm introduces a different angle by making predictions based on the proximity of data points. KNN operates on the assumption that similar things exist in close proximity, measuring distances between data points using various metrics like Euclidean distance. This intuitive approach is easy to understand and implement, making it ideal for practical applications such as recommendation systems or market segmentation. Consider a music streaming service recommending songs; KNN analyzes user preferences and listens history to suggest tracks enjoyed by others with similar tastes. Despite its simplicity, KNN is powerful in scenarios where interpretability and ease of implementation outweigh the need for speed, especially with smaller datasets.

Together, these algorithms form a robust toolkit for understanding and utilizing machine learning in real-world situations. They provide a roadmap for learners, from novices to seasoned professionals, each offering unique strengths tailored to specific tasks. Whether predicting future sales, classifying images, or suggesting personalized content, these algorithms are fundamental in navigating the ever-evolving landscape of artificial intelligence.

The Role of Data in Training Models

Data plays a critical role in the realm of machine learning, serving as the foundation upon which models are built and predictions are made. Ensuring data is both high-quality and abundant is paramount for achieving accurate results and optimizing model performance. Let's explore why these elements matter and how they contribute to successful machine learning applications.

First and foremost, the quality of data has a direct impact on how well a model performs. When data is reliable, clean, and relevant, it enhances a model's ability to learn and make precise predictions. High-quality data eliminates noise and inaccuracies that could otherwise lead to errors in output. For example, if a dataset contains incorrect labels or missing values, a machine learning model may learn incorrect patterns, leading to faulty decision-making processes. By prioritizing data quality through practices such as data cleansing and validation, we improve the chances of our models delivering consistent and accurate results.

Equally important is the quantity of data available for training machine learning models. The volume of data affects the learning process significantly. Too little data can lead to challenges with underfitting, where the model fails to capture the underlying trends and complexity of the data. Conversely, an overwhelming amount of data might cause overfitting, where a model memorizes the training data instead of generalizing from it. Striking the right balance in data volume is thus essential. For instance, in developing a predictive model for customer behavior, having just enough historical transaction data can help identify meaningful patterns without being bogged down by noise.

A crucial step in ensuring both data quality and optimal volume is feature selection. This process involves identifying and selecting those features within a dataset that are most informative and relevant for the task at hand. By focusing on these key features, the model's accuracy improves because it's trained on more pertinent information rather than extraneous or redundant data. Take image classification, for instance, where the inclusion of features like object shapes and colors is vital, while dismissing irrelevant data such as background noise enhances prediction accuracy. Feature selection techniques, like forward selection or recursive feature elimination, help streamline this process, refining the data fed into models.

Moreover, effective data management strategies play a pivotal role in streamlining data handling and organization, further enhancing model performance. Data management encapsulates the collection, storage, and maintenance of data, ensuring it's readily accessible and up-to-date. Utilizing organizational tools like data warehouses and cloud storage solutions helps manage large datasets efficiently, reducing delays and potential bottlenecks during analysis. In business intelligence, leveraging robust data management systems facilitates seamless integration and retrieval of data across departments, supporting informed decision-making and strategy development.

To address the challenges associated with data quality and quantity, organizations should implement guidelines that ensure systematic data collection and processing methods. A comprehensive data governance framework outlines procedures for data acquisition, outlines

24

responsibilities, and sets standards for data integrity. Regular audits and assessments of data sources and their quality help maintain standards, preventing issues before they arise. Transparent documentation of data lineage, or the history of each dataset, also offers insights into its origins and transformations, aiding in troubleshooting errors and ensuring compliance with regulations.

Additionally, integrating automated data preprocessing techniques can assist in maintaining data standards and preparing it for modeling. Techniques such as normalization and standardization help scale and align data points for consistency across datasets. Automation minimizes manual intervention, reducing human error and increasing efficiency in data preparation workflows. For instance, automating the detection and removal of duplicates in sales data ensures accuracy and clarity, allowing marketing teams to target customers effectively.

It's also crucial to foster collaboration between data scientists, domain experts, and IT professionals to harness the full potential of data in machine learning endeavors. Open communication channels and regular meetings promote a shared understanding of data requirements, objectives, and constraints among team members. By collaborating closely, teams can anticipate data-related challenges early on and devise tailored solutions that enhance data quality and availability.

Overfitting and Model Evaluation

In the journey of mastering machine learning, one of the key challenges encountered is overfitting. It's an issue that arises when a model performs exceptionally well on training data but struggles to generalize its learnings to new, unseen data. Imagine crafting a study guide so perfect for a specific test that it becomes essentially useless for any other scenario. This is because the model, like the over-prepared student, has memorized the answers rather than understanding the underlying principles.

Overfitting can occur due to several factors, such as using overly complex models with too many parameters relative to the amount of available data. These models might capture noise and peculiarities in the training set instead of identifying overarching patterns or trends. The implications of overfitting are significant: a model that cannot generalize will likely produce inaccurate predictions when faced with real-world data, ultimately undermining the reliability and utility of the machine learning system.

To understand whether a model is overfitting, it's essential to employ model evaluation metrics. These metrics provide a quantitative basis for assessing model performance. Accuracy, for instance, measures how often the model makes correct predictions across the entire dataset. While accuracy is straightforward, it may not always tell the whole story. In scenarios where class distribution is imbalanced, precision and recall become more informative. Precision quantifies the number of true positive results divided by the sum of true positives and false positives, indicating how many selected items are relevant. Recall (or sensitivity) calculates the number of true positive results divided by the sum of true positives and false negatives, showing how many relevant items were selected. The F1 score harmonizes precision and recall into a single metric, offering a balance between these two aspects when neither can be sacrificed for the sake of the other.

Using these metrics helps in understanding not only if but how and where a model is failing. However, relying solely on them might not fully prevent overfitting. This is where cross-validation techniques become valuable. Cross-validation involves dividing the dataset into subsets, training the model on some of these subsets known as training sets, and validating it on the remaining ones. By repeatedly rotating through different data segments, cross-validation ensures that every part of the dataset has been used for both training and validation, thus providing a more comprehensive assessment of the model's performance.

One popular method of cross-validation is k-fold cross-validation. Here, the original dataset is randomly partitioned into k equal-sized subsamples. Out of these k subsamples, a single subsample is retained as the validation data for testing the model, and the remaining k-1 subsamples are used as training data. This process is then repeated k times, with each of the k subsamples used exactly once as the validation data. The results from the folds can then be averaged to produce a single estimation. By providing various perspectives on model performance, cross-validation improves reliability and reduces the risk of overfitting.

Beyond these methods, practical strategies exist within iterative improvement and testing cycles. Continuous iteration allows for incremental enhancement of models, honing their ability to generalize better with each cycle. Begin by testing a model on a training set, evaluating its performance using the aforementioned metrics, and identifying areas where the model fails. Based on this analysis, adjust the model parameters, fine-tune algorithms, or introduce regularization techniques that penalize complexity to minimize potential overfitting. Repeat the evaluation and adjustment processes, iterating until you achieve a balanced model capable of performing effectively on new data.

In practice, a strategic combination of these approaches often proves most effective. Start with a simple model to set a baseline. Gradually introduce complexity as dictated by the performance assessments. Always consider the domain-specific nature of the data being handled, as certain datasets might inherently require more sophisticated tactics due to their intrinsic variability or dimensionality.

Choosing the Right Method

When embarking on a machine learning project, one of the most critical decisions involves selecting the appropriate learning method. This choice largely hinges upon understanding whether supervised or unsupervised learning best fits your specific situation. Each learning type has unique characteristics that suit different kinds of problems, so assessing the context is vital. Supervised learning requires labeled data, meaning each input comes with a known output. It's typically used for tasks where predictions are necessary, such as identifying spam emails or predicting house prices. On the other hand, unsupervised learning works with unlabeled data, seeking to uncover hidden patterns or structures without specific outputs in mind. This method excels in clustering similar data points or reducing dimensionality to make sense of complex datasets.

To choose wisely between these two methods, it's essential to develop and apply critical thinking skills. Analyzing the types of data you possess and the outcomes you aim to achieve can guide your strategy in significant ways. For instance, if your dataset consists of customer purchase histories and you want to predict future buying behavior, supervised learning might be more appropriate because the data includes past interactions with defined outcomes. However, if your goal is to segment customers into distinct groups based on purchasing habits, an unsupervised approach like clustering algorithms would likely yield better insights.

Understanding the relationship between project goals and data availability also plays a pivotal role in successful implementation. Consider a scenario where a company wants to enhance its recommendation system but has limited user interaction data. The scarcity of labeled data may compel a shift towards unsupervised techniques that don't rely heavily on predefined labels. By clearly defining what success looks like for your project—whether it's improving prediction accuracy, discovering new patterns, or enhancing operational efficiency—and aligning this with the data at hand, you can streamline your approach to deploying machine learning effectively.

Selection frameworks offer valuable guidance in navigating these complex decisions, helping refine the process of choosing appropriate machine learning methods. These frameworks often provide structured approaches that simplify the selection process, breaking down the decision-making into logical steps or criteria that emphasize alignment with project objectives and available resources. Such frameworks might involve evaluating the complexity of algorithms, the scalability of solutions, or the interpretability of results. They help ensure that all potential strategies are considered and rationally assessed against current needs and constraints.

Moreover, effective frameworks highlight the importance of feature selection and data management as part of refining your methodological choices. Feature selection—a process that identifies the most informative attributes within your data set—helps improve model performance by eliminating redundancy while focusing on the aspects that truly influence outcomes. Concentrating on key features not only enhances the efficiency of learning algorithms but also reduces computational costs and speeds up processing times. Incorporating guidelines for feature selection within your framework ensures models remain robust and less prone to overfitting.

Effective data management strategies further complement the selection framework, providing a foundation for handling vast amounts of information efficiently. From organizing and maintaining data integrity to ensuring accessibility and security, good data management practices keep the entire analytical process streamlined and error-free. These strategies facilitate smooth transitions between different analytical models and learning methods as needed, adapting to shifts in project requirements or data landscapes.

CHAPTER 3

Demystifying Neural Networks

U nderstanding neural networks is crucial in the realm of artificial intelligence, as they serve as the backbone for numerous AI technologies. These intricate systems are designed to replicate the way a human brain processes information, drawing inspiration from our own biological structures. This connection to cognitive processes allows them to tackle problems and tasks once thought impossible for machines. The allure of neural networks lies in how they emulate learning and decision-making capabilities akin to human thinking, offering a glimpse into the future possibilities of machine intelligence. For many, these networks represent a complex blend of computer science and neuroscience, merging to form a new frontier in technology that promises to revolutionize various sectors.

In this chapter, readers will delve into the components of neural networks and their function within AI technology. The journey begins with an exploration of the neuron, the foundational building block, often likened to brain cells. From there, the chapter will guide through the architecture of neural networks, detailing the input, hidden, and output layers that define its structure. Additionally, it will cover the critical role played by connections between neurons, known as synapses, and how weights and biases influence the network's capability to learn from data. By dissecting these elements, the chapter aims to demystify the workings of neural networks, making them accessible to beginners while offering valuable insights for professionals and educators seeking to enhance their understanding of AI systems.

Structure of Neural Networks

To understand the intricate workings of neural networks, one must first explore their foundational element: the neuron. Often compared to brain cells, neurons in a neural network serve as fundamental processing units that transform input data into output. This conversion can be likened to basic decision-making processes where information is evaluated and results are produced. Think of a neuron as a tiny decision-making machine; it assesses the data it receives, weighs its importance, and then produces an outcome based on predefined rules or learned experiences. This mirroring of human cognitive processes not only simplifies complex operations but also lays the groundwork for more advanced learning systems.

Expanding the landscape of neural networks reveals their structured composition consisting of multiple layers, namely input, hidden, and output layers. Each of these components plays a crucial role in shaping the capabilities of the network. The input layer acts as the entry point for data, receiving raw information that needs processing. Once received, the data then traverses through hidden layers, which are pivotal for organizing and analyzing patterns. These hidden layers are akin to a processing hub where the actual 'thinking' happens, allowing the network to learn and adapt by recognizing intricate patterns within the data. Finally, the output layer presents the end result, synthesizing all previous computations into a comprehensible format. This layered architecture ensures efficient data organization and boosts the network's capacity for pattern recognition, enabling applications from image recognition to language translation.

Integral to the function of these networks are the connections between neurons, known as synapses, which possess adjustable weights. During training sessions, these weights are modified to refine the accuracy of predictions made by the network. By adjusting these weights, the network learns to give preferential treatment to certain inputs over others, enhancing its ability to forecast with increasing precision. Imagine a network being taught to identify handwritten digits; initially, it might struggle, but as it practices, the weight adjustments allow it to discern subtle differences between a '3' and an '8'. This progressive refinement underscores the adaptive nature of neural networks and their potential for improved predictive performance.

Alongside weights, bias parameters are another critical element facilitating enhanced pattern recognition. Bias parameters shift the activation functions of neurons, making them more adept at identifying complex and non-linear patterns. Consider bias as a form of calibration that fine-tunes the activation thresholds, allowing the network to accommodate variation within input data more effectively. This adjustment improves the network's overall flexibility, ensuring it responds appropriately to diverse inputs. For instance, when a neural network faces ambiguous or overlapping classes during tasks like facial recognition, biases help in navigating these complexities, thus elevating the accuracy of the final output.

In illustration, picture a scenario where a neural network is trained to differentiate between cats and dogs in images. Here, each neuron processes elements such as fur texture, ear shape, and tail length. The input layer absorbs pixel values, transmitting them to hidden layers where these features are dissected further. Weights between neurons would prioritize specific characteristics depending on the outcome of prior learning sessions—perhaps emphasizing texture over color. Simultaneously, biases might help the network account for instances where lighting changes affect perception, allowing consistent identification regardless of varying conditions.

Activation Functions Explained

The crucial role of activation functions within neural networks cannot be overstated. These functions are the gatekeepers that determine whether a neuron should activate, allowing it to pass information along the network. The introduction of non-linearity through activation functions enhances the network's ability to learn complex patterns and representations.

At the heart of activation functions is their critical task of deciding which neurons to fire, based on the inputs they receive. This decision-making process allows neural networks to understand and model intricate relationships in data, moving beyond simple linear mappings. Without this ability to induce non-linearity, neural networks would be limited in their capacity to process complex real-world data.

Various types of activation functions have been designed over time, each serving distinct purposes and influencing the learning process differently. One popular type is the Sigmoid function, which maps input values to an output range between zero and one. This characteristic makes it particularly useful for binary classification tasks where outputs are confined to two classes. However, the Sigmoid function can suffer from gradient saturation at extreme values, slowing down learning when gradients become nearly zero.

Another widely-used activation function is ReLU (Rectified Linear Unit), which has become an industry standard for many deep learning applications. By returning the input directly if it's positive and zero otherwise, ReLU introduces sufficient non-linearity without capping the potential growth of node activations. This feature enables fast and efficient training by mitigating the vanishing gradient problem often encountered with Sigmoid functions, thereby accelerating convergence during optimization.

The Tanh function, a hyperbolic tangent activation, offers a middle ground. It scales inputs to outputs ranging from minus one to one, effectively centralizing the activations around zero. Like the Sigmoid, it also suffers from the vanishing gradient issue but generally performs better due to its symmetric nature. Tanh is especially effective when dealing with features exhibiting strong negative signals, offering a smooth gradient that aids in model training.

Selecting the appropriate activation function impacts not only the speed but also the efficiency of neural network training. For instance, while Sigmoid might be ideal for simpler models or low-risk applications, more complex scenarios might benefit from the computational efficiency and robustness provided by ReLU. This choice affects how quickly a model can learn from the data and reach optimal performance levels.

The learning process in neural networks heavily relies on mechanisms like gradient descent and backpropagation. Activation functions play an indispensable role here, as they influence how errors are propagated back through the layers to adjust weights and biases. During learning, neurons update their connections based on the gradients calculated from the loss function. If an activation function results in very small gradients, as seen in the saturation zones of Sigmoid and Tanh, this gradient flow can hinder the learning process, slowing down or even stalling network training.

ReLU addresses some of these issues by maintaining a stronger gradient presence throughout the network, which is crucial for effective weight updates. This clear gradient path ensures that all layers of the network receive meaningful error feedback, enabling them to contribute actively to refining the model. Consequently, networks utilizing ReLU can achieve higher accuracy with fewer iterations compared to those relying solely on Sigmoid or Tanh functions.

While ReLU has its advantages, it isn't perfect. Its tendency to produce dead neurons—neurons that no longer activate across any dataset samples— poses challenges. Once a neuron is switched off due to consistent negative inputs, it may never recover, potentially reducing model capacity. Solutions such as Leaky ReLU, which assigns a small slope to negative inputs, help address this issue by keeping neurons alive, thus preserving learning potential across all parts of the network.

Training a Neural Network: Backpropagation

In the realm of artificial intelligence, neural networks stand out as powerful tools that mimic the human brain's capacity for learning. A crucial component of this learning process is backpropagation, a method indispensable to training neural networks effectively. To grasp how backpropagation functions, we must first understand its primary role: calculating loss gradients and updating weights in the network.

At the heart of any learning algorithm is the concept of minimizing errors or "loss." When a neural network makes predictions, these predictions are compared to actual outcomes using a loss function, a mathematical formula that quantifies the difference between predicted and true values. Backpropagation uses this difference to calculate the gradient of the loss function with respect to each weight in the network. By doing so, it identifies how small changes in weights affect the overall error. This information is pivotal because it guides the adjustments made to the network's weights during training, steering the system closer to accurate predictions.

The learning process can be divided into two phases: the forward pass and the backward pass. During the forward pass, inputs progress through layers of neurons to produce an output. This output is then evaluated against expected results using the chosen loss function. Once the loss is determined, the backward pass begins. Here, backpropagation comes into play by computing gradients—the partial derivatives of the loss with respect to each weight—through a process called reverse-mode differentiation. This step is vital as it informs how each weight in the network should be adjusted to reduce error most efficiently.

Understanding the dual nature of this process is essential. The forward pass essentially computes the outcome based on current parameters, while the backward pass refines those parameters—weights—using detailed feedback from the error gradients. Together, these passes create a continuous loop of prediction and adjustment, propelling the network towards higher accuracy over time.

Central to this optimization process is the selection of an appropriate loss function. The choice of loss function can significantly impact how well the network learns. For instance, Mean Squared Error (MSE) is commonly used for regression tasks, where the goal is to predict continuous values. On the other hand, classification tasks—where outputs fall into distinct categories—often employ cross-entropy loss. Each function serves a specific purpose, aligning the network's learning algorithm with the desired outcome, whether predicting house prices, classifying images, or performing any number of AI-driven tasks.

Yet, even with effective loss functions and precise calculations, backpropagation would still falter without another key element: the learning rate. The learning rate controls the size of updates applied to the network's weights during training. Setting this parameter involves a careful trade-off. A high learning rate may speed up training by making large corrective steps, but it risks overshooting the optimal solution, leading to unstable or oscillating learning patterns. Conversely, a low learning rate ensures more stable convergence but can make training painfully slow, as it takes smaller steps toward minimizing loss.

Striking the right balance with the learning rate is crucial for maintaining training efficiency without sacrificing stability. Often, practitioners employ techniques like learning rate schedules, which adjust the learning rate dynamically throughout training, or adaptive learning rate methods such as Adam and RMSprop. These approaches fine-tune the learning rate in response to the network's training progression, enhancing both speed and precision.

As backpropagation orchestrates these elements—loss gradients, weight updates, forward and backward passes, appropriate loss functions, and balanced learning rates—it becomes clear why it's hailed as the backbone of neural networks. Despite the complexity inherent in this process, understanding its fundamentals empowers individuals across various fields to harness the power of AI more effectively.

For beginners, recognizing backpropagation's systematic approach demystifies what might initially seem like a black box. Professionals seeking to improve their skills can appreciate the precision involved in tuning these systems for better performance. Educators gain a structured narrative to impart foundational AI concepts to students, preparing them for future careers. Meanwhile, STEM students can see how theoretical knowledge directly applies to practical challenges in AI.

Moreover, by illuminating the components of backpropagation, this discussion offers insight into the broader question of how machines learn and make decisions. It underscores the importance of each step in achieving effective learning in neural networks and lays the groundwork for deeper exploration into more advanced topics in artificial intelligence.

Applications of Neural Networks: Image Recognition and NLP

Neural networks have become a cornerstone of artificial intelligence, powering applications that might have seemed like science fiction not long ago. Among the most fascinating uses of neural networks is image recognition, a technology that allows computers to interpret and understand visual data much like humans do. This capability stems from the way neural networks are designed to mimic the human brain's ability to process various types of signals. When we look at an image, our brains quickly identify and categorize objects within it by recognizing patterns. Similarly, in image recognition, neural networks are trained on large datasets containing millions of labeled images. They learn to detect patterns, edges, and textures, enabling them to recognize objects with remarkable accuracy.

The power of image recognition is evident in countless real-world scenarios. Take your smartphone, for example. Facial recognition technology uses neural networks to allow you to unlock your device simply by looking at it. Beyond personal gadgets, these systems are employed in security applications, where they can scan surveillance footage to detect suspicious activities or specific individuals. Retail environments use image recognition to track inventory levels or monitor customer behavior, helping businesses optimize their operations.

Another transformative application of neural networks is in Natural Language Processing (NLP), which facilitates interaction between humans and machines using natural language. NLP enables machines to perform tasks such as translation, sentiment analysis, and even conversation generation. A chatbot, driven by NLP, can understand user queries and provide responses in a way that mimics human communication. This technology relies heavily on neural networks, which analyze linguistic data, learning from vast corpora of texts to discern patterns and relationships in language.

Consider the global reach of NLP technology. Language translation systems like Google Translate harness neural networks to convert text from one language to another, facilitating communication across the world's diverse linguistic landscape. In customer service, chatbots powered by NLP handle routine inquiries, leaving human agents free to tackle more complex issues. By transforming raw text into structured data that computers can work with, NLP applications expand the possibilities for automation and personalization.

A crucial aspect of both image recognition and NLP is the demonstration of AI's capacity for generating human-like responses. Neural networks allow systems to not only process but also generate novel content, leading to more interactive and intuitive engagements. For instance, voice assistants like Siri or Alexa rely on NLP to understand user commands and respond appropriately, often employing sophisticated algorithms to predict user needs and preferences over time.

Real-world examples vividly illustrate the practical impacts of these technologies. In the tech industry, companies like Tesla deploy neural networks in their self-driving cars, integrating image recognition to navigate roads safely by identifying obstacles and traffic signs. Meanwhile, Amazon uses NLP in its recommendation systems to analyze customer reviews and improve product suggestions, heightening the shopping experience.

These applications go beyond enhancing convenience—they illuminate AI's potential to reshape industries. The inclusion of image recognition and NLP in sectors such as healthcare implies a future where machines assist doctors by interpreting medical images or offer patients mental health support through empathetic virtual therapy sessions. In education, smart tutoring systems powered by NLP can tailor instruction to meet individual student needs, improving learning outcomes.

Applications of Neural Networks: Healthcare and Financial Services

Neural networks, a fundamental component of artificial intelligence technology, are making significant strides in transforming various sectors. Particularly in healthcare and finance, these advanced systems are revolutionizing how we diagnose diseases, predict health outcomes, and manage financial operations.

In the realm of healthcare, neural networks assist in diagnosing diseases with a level of accuracy that was previously unattainable. By analyzing vast amounts of medical data, they can identify patterns that may be invisible to the human eye. For instance, neural networks have been employed to interpret medical imaging, such as MRIs and X-rays, leading to early detection of conditions like cancer. The ability to quickly and accurately process this information means that patients can receive diagnoses earlier, which is crucial for successful treatment outcomes. Furthermore, predicting health outcomes is another area where neural networks show great promise. By assessing patient histories and statistical data, AI models can forecast potential health risks, enabling proactive management and personalized treatment plans that could greatly improve patient care and streamline hospital operations.

In finance, the impact of neural networks is equally transformative. These systems enhance financial services by playing a critical role in fraud detection, risk assessment, and market predictions. Fraud detection, for example, involves real-time analysis of transactions to identify unusual patterns or anomalies that might suggest fraudulent activity. Neural networks learn from vast datasets, including historical transaction records, to distinguish between normal and suspicious behavior, thus protecting consumers and businesses from financial losses. Risk assessment benefits from similar capabilities, allowing institutions to better evaluate the probability of default on loans and credit lines. By factoring in numerous variables, neural networks provide more comprehensive risk profiles than traditional methods. In terms of market predictions, AI leverages complex algorithms to analyze market trends and predict future movements, offering valuable insights that can guide investment strategies and business decisions.

Across both healthcare and finance, AI applications offer improvements in operational efficiencies and decision-making processes, especially in high-stakes situations. In healthcare, this means streamlining administrative tasks, reducing redundancy, and optimizing resource allocation, which allows healthcare professionals to focus more on patient care rather than paperwork. Similarly, in finance, AI-driven automation reduces manual processing times, enhances customer service through swift query handling, and improves regulatory compliance by monitoring changes in real-time and alerting relevant stakeholders.

Case studies elucidate the societal relevance and potential of neural networks across industries. One striking example is IBM's Watson, used in various hospitals to aid in oncology. Watson analyzes a patient's medical history in conjunction with rapidly evolving medical literature to propose tailored treatment options. This not only democratizes specialist knowledge but also ensures that treatments are based on the most current research. In finance, companies like JPMorgan Chase use neural networks to optimize trading strategies and manage vast portfolios effectively, showcasing the immense potential for boosting economic activities at scale.

While neural networks significantly contribute to these fields, their implications extend beyond operational enhancements. They represent a paradigm shift towards data-driven decision-making, challenging industries to rethink traditional processes. For example, in healthcare, the integration of neural networks encourages a shift towards preventative care rather than reactive treatment, emphasizing wellness and long-term health management. Similarly, in finance, predictive analytics foster a culture of anticipatory strategy formulation, guiding firms towards stability and growth.

As we explore the transformative effects of neural networks in healthcare diagnostics and finance, it's essential to remain aware of their challenges and limitations. Issues such as data privacy, ethical considerations, and the need for transparency in AI decision-making processes continue to spark discussions among professionals and policymakers. Ensuring that AI applications are used responsibly will be key to harnessing their full potential while safeguarding individual rights and maintaining public trust.

CHAPTER 4

Diving into Generative AI

U nderstanding generative AI is an essential step for anyone interested in the evolution of technology and its impact on creativity and innovation. This chapter delves into the concept of generative AI, which stands apart from traditional AI due to its unique ability to create new content rather than merely processing existing data. Its role transcends various fields, offering novel approaches to solve complex problems and enhance creative processes. As generative AI progresses, it opens doors to possibilities once considered exclusive to human imagination.

Throughout this chapter, readers will learn about the foundational elements that make generative AI a game-changer in today's digital landscape. The discussion highlights how this technology generates new art, music, text, and even fresh ideas across multiple industries. By exploring the mechanics behind this form of artificial intelligence, the chapter provides insights into how algorithms can craft outputs with distinct originality. Furthermore, practical examples illustrate the profound implications of generative AI in domains such as entertainment, design, and technology. These discussions aim to equip beginners, professionals, educators, and students with a comprehensive understanding of how generative AI is reshaping their fields. The chapter emphasizes the strategic blending of human creativity with AI-generated innovations, showing how this synergy enhances productivity without diminishing the value of human intuition and artistic flair.

What is Generative AI?

Generative AI represents a fascinating and rapidly evolving branch of artificial intelligence that focuses on creating new and original content. Unlike traditional AI, which is primarily engaged in processing and analyzing existing data to deliver insights or automate tasks, generative AI stands out due to its remarkable ability to generate entirely new data. This capability extends far beyond mere replication, enabling the creation of novel works that can sometimes rival the creativity and uniqueness of human efforts.

At its core, generative AI encompasses a variety of algorithms designed to produce content from scratch. These algorithms are not limited to specific types of content; they can create images, compose music, develop text, and even come up with fresh concepts. This breadth of functionality illustrates the transformative potential of generative AI, fundamentally altering how we think about creativity in the digital age. With advanced machine learning models, generative AI can explore vast creative possibilities, pushing boundaries and redefining what machines can accomplish.

One of the key differentiators of generative AI from traditional AI systems lies in its ability to make something new rather than simply process what already exists. Traditional AI excels at sifting through large datasets to find patterns or make predictions. In contrast, generative AI takes a step further by producing outputs that have never been seen before, showcasing its role as both an assistant and a pioneer in innovative processes. For instance, instead of merely analyzing thousands of art pieces to identify trends, generative AI might create an entirely new style of artwork that reflects those trends while adding unique elements.

This ability to generate new data rather than just analyze existing data is a significant leap forward in artificial intelligence development. It marks a transition from using AI as a tool for enhancing efficiency to employing it as a partner in creativity. The implications for innovation are profound, as this technology paves the way for developing original ideas and artifacts across multiple domains. A guideline for leveraging this capability effectively involves blending human creativity with AI-generated inputs, ensuring that the synergy between man and machine enhances rather than replaces human intuition and artistic vision.

The versatility of generative AI is evident across various industries. In entertainment, for example, generative AI algorithms have been utilized to develop scripts, compose music, and create visual effects that would be labor-intensive if created manually. This approach not only speeds up the production process but also allows for more experimentation and iteration, ultimately leading to more nuanced and diverse creative outputs. In technology, generative AI contributes to software development by automatically writing code snippets, designing user interfaces, and optimizing system performance. This assistance can enhance productivity, allowing developers to focus on higher-level problem-solving and strategic planning.

Art is another area experiencing significant transformation due to generative AI. Artists and designers harness these algorithms to push creative boundaries, exploring styles and formats previously unattainable without technological aid. Generative AI tools enable artists to visualize complex patterns and experiment with forms and colors, thus broadening their creative horizons. This fusion of art and technology encourages a dynamic exchange of ideas, where machines and humans collaboratively influence the evolution of artistic expression.

In the world of architecture and design, generative AI plays a crucial role in crafting innovative and sustainable structures. By simulating countless design iterations, these tools help architects optimize form and function, considering factors such as energy efficiency, material use, and aesthetic appeal. The results are often groundbreaking designs that balance beauty with practicality, exemplifying how generative AI contributes to solving real-world challenges while elevating creative standards.

Additionally, generative AI's ability to personalize experiences is transforming customer engagement in various sectors. Retailers, for example, utilize AI-generated recommendations to offer custom shopping experiences tailored to individual preferences. Similarly, in gaming, generative algorithms create adaptive game environments and narratives that respond to player actions, enhancing immersion and replayability. This adaptability highlights the potential of generative AI to revolutionize user interaction, making experiences more engaging and relevant.

Generative AI also opens new avenues in education by developing personalized learning materials and interactive simulations that cater to different learning styles and rates. Educators can leverage these tools to create customized curricula that address students' unique needs, potentially improving educational outcomes by providing targeted support and resources. This integration of AI into education demonstrates its capacity to transform traditional teaching methods and foster a more inclusive and effective learning environment.

Introduction to GANs (Generative Adversarial Networks)

Generative Adversarial Networks (GANs) are a fundamental technology in the realm of generative AI. They have drastically reshaped creativity and innovation across various fields by harnessing the power of deep learning. At the core of GAN architecture lies a unique symbiotic operation between two neural networks: the generator and the discriminator.

The generator's role is to produce data that mimic real-world examples, such as crafting images or creating voice samples that appear authentic.

Simultaneously, the discriminator stands as a gatekeeper, evaluating the output from the generator against real data and distinguishing between the two. This dynamic creates a fascinating interplay where both networks continuously improve through a process akin to a competitive game. As the generator gets better at faking reality, the discriminator becomes adept at detecting these forgeries, leading to both networks honing their capabilities.

Training GANs effectively is no small feat and showcases the complexity inherent in AI technologies. The success of this training hinges on achieving a delicate balance between the generator and discriminator. If either network overpowers the other, it can lead to suboptimal outcomes—a scenario known as mode collapse, where the generator produces limited varieties of outputs, failing to capture diversity. To counteract such challenges, practitioners employ sophisticated techniques like adjusting learning rates or deploying advanced optimization algorithms.

The applications of GANs span multiple domains, marking significant technological advancements. A prominent example is realistic image generation, where GANs can create hyper-realistic art or synthetic imagery used in media and entertainment. Similarly, lifelike voice synthesis is revolutionizing fields such as virtual assistants and dubbing in films, providing natural-sounding speech that humans find indistinguishable from real recordings. These applications not only enhance user experiences but also prompt discussions about the nature of art and authenticity.

Looking ahead, future trends in GAN development suggest continually evolving capabilities. Innovations in GAN architecture and training methods promise even more sophisticated outputs. For instance, researchers are exploring GAN variations capable of generating 3D models and complex animations, pushing boundaries in gaming and augmented reality. Additionally, advancements in computational power and algorithms are likely to reduce the time required for training, enabling quicker iterations and broader accessibility.

Use Cases of Generative Models

Generative AI is transforming industries by introducing innovative approaches and reshaping traditional methods. In media and entertainment, it has become a game-changer, contributing to the development of AI-generated scripts and artwork that challenge conventional creative processes. Filmmakers and scriptwriters are exploring AI's potential to generate fresh storylines and dialogues, allowing for quicker production times and innovative content. For instance, AI can analyze vast amounts of existing scripts and create new narratives with unique twists. Similarly, digital artists employ AI to generate intricate artwork that combines various styles, pushing the boundaries of creativity.

To ensure effective implementation of generative models in media and entertainment, creators should integrate these tools as collaborative aids rather than replacements for human creativity. Encouraging a synergy between human intuition and AI capabilities will likely lead to richer and more diverse artistic outputs. Additionally, practitioners should remain vigilant about ethical considerations, ensuring that AI-generated content maintains authenticity and respects intellectual property laws.

In the field of design and architecture, generative models have prompted a revolution by enabling rapid design variations. Architects and designers use AI to produce multiple iterations of a single concept quickly, fostering innovation in form and function. This capability not only accelerates the design process but also allows for more exploratory phases, where designers can assess numerous options before settling on a final blueprint. In urban planning, AI helps visualize cityscapes, offering detailed simulations that assist in decision-making processes regarding infrastructure and aesthetics.

When utilizing generative models in design and architecture, professionals should emphasize iterative feedback loops. By continuously refining AI-generated designs based on user feedback, practitioners can enhance both functionality and aesthetic appeal. Moreover, incorporating diverse data sources into AI systems will result in more culturally inclusive designs, broadening the impact of architectural innovations.

The healthcare sector is also witnessing remarkable advancements thanks to generative AI, particularly in drug development and medical research. Generative models contribute to the generation of novel data sets, which accelerate the discovery of new drugs and treatment protocols. By simulating complex biological processes, AI can predict how different compounds interact, streamlining the path from discovery to clinical trials. Researchers benefit from AI's ability to analyze large volumes of biomedical data, uncovering insights that might otherwise go unnoticed.

While explicit guidelines are less critical in healthcare applications, it's crucial to maintain robust collaboration among researchers, clinicians, and AI developers. Such collaborations ensure that AI model outcomes align with practical medical needs and improve patient care. Consistent evaluation and validation of AI predictions against empirical data will reinforce trust in these technologies and facilitate their integration into routine clinical workflows.

In gaming, generative AI creates dynamic and immersive user experiences by enhancing interactive environments. Game developers leverage AI models to generate rich content, such as NPC (non-player character) behavior, plot developments, and level designs, all tailored to individual player interactions. This personalization results in games that adapt to the player's style, making each experience unique and engaging. The sophistication of AI-generated worlds captivates players and offers endless opportunities for exploration and enjoyment.

To optimize generative AI in gaming, developers should focus on balancing autonomy and control within AI systems. Allowing AI to generate diverse scenarios while maintaining narrative coherence ensures that player engagement remains high. Furthermore, promoting transparency in AI decisions will help build player trust and acceptance of AI-driven game elements.

Challenges and Ethics in Generative AI

In the realm of generative AI, ethical considerations hold significant weight as these technologies influence multiple aspects of our society. One primary area of concern is the emergence of biases during model training. Bias can infiltrate AI systems because they learn patterns from existing data, which might reflect societal prejudices. For example, if a model is trained on datasets that contain biased information about a group of people, it may produce outputs that perpetuate or even amplify those biases. This situation poses ethical dilemmas when AI solutions are applied, potentially leading to unfair treatment of individuals or groups in various applications like hiring processes, law enforcement, or media representation.

Identifying and addressing these biases is crucial to creating fair and equitable AI systems. Developers must carefully select and preprocess training data to minimize biases, while also implementing rigorous testing and evaluation procedures. Transparency in the data used and the methodologies followed can help ensure more ethical outcomes. Collaboration with diverse teams can also foster systems less prone to narrow viewpoints, promoting inclusivity and fairness.

Another challenge lies in the misuse of generative AI, particularly through technologies like deepfakes, which illustrate the potential for malicious use. Deepfake technology enables the creation of highly realistic but fabricated audio-visual content, presenting risks for misinformation and personal harm. For instance, deepfakes could be employed to undermine political figures by altering speeches or creating false events, thereby influencing public opinion and electoral outcomes. They could also be used to fabricate compromising videos of individuals, damaging reputations and causing psychological distress.

The potential for such misuse underscores the necessity of establishing stringent ethical standards as well as technological solutions for identification and accountability. Detection tools that can accurately distinguish between genuine and artificially generated content are vital in combating malicious use. Moreover, legal frameworks need to be strengthened to address the unauthorized creation and distribution of deepfakes, offering protection to victims and providing deterrents to unethical actors.

Legal and copyright issues also surface when discussing AI-generated content ownership, prompting complex intellectual property discussions. The question arises: Who owns the output created by an AI? Is it the developer who designed the model, the entity that provided the input data, or the user who directed the AI's application? These questions complicate the traditional understanding of authorship and ownership, especially in creative industries where generative AI can produce music, art, and literature reminiscent of human creators.

Guidelines must be established to navigate these legalities, ensuring the rights of creators are protected while also considering the contributions made by AI technologies. Collaborative efforts among developers, legal experts, and policymakers are essential to formulating comprehensive policies that address these emerging issues. Furthermore, education around these topics should be promoted within industries reliant on generative AI to prepare all stakeholders for navigating these complex waters.

Establishing ethical guidelines involves collaboration among developers, researchers, and industry leaders to cultivate responsible technologies. This collaboration is fundamental in shaping frameworks that dictate how AI should be developed and utilized across different sectors. For example, leading tech companies and academic institutions might team up to draft ethical codes of conduct that prioritize transparency, accountability, and fairness in AI development. Such guidelines should not only consider current capabilities but also anticipate future advancements and the unprecedented challenges they may present.

Training programs and workshops focusing on ethical AI practices can facilitate a deeper understanding among developers and users alike, equipping them with the skills needed to evaluate and mitigate potential harms. As the landscape of AI continues to evolve, adapting ethical standards to meet new developments will be crucial in maintaining the integrity and trustworthiness of AI technologies.

Real-World Examples and Implications

Generative AI has emerged as a transformative force in various fields, offering innovative applications that reshape traditional creative and technological processes. Two of the most prominent examples illustrating generative AI's capabilities are AI-generated artwork and deepfake technology. These technologies not only exemplify the core principles of generative AI but also underscore its broader implications for creativity and innovation.

AI-generated artwork is a fascinating development that showcases how machines can create visually stunning images that rival human artists' creations. Artists and technologists have harnessed algorithms known as neural networks to generate these artworks, resulting in pieces that often provoke thought and evoke emotion. The process involves training a model on a vast array of existing art styles and forms. Once trained, the model can produce new art by combining learned patterns uniquely. One notable example is the portrait "Edmond de Belamy," created by the Paris-based art collective Obvious. When auctioned at Christie's, it fetched an impressive $432,500, highlighting the growing interest and value in AI-generated art.

Deepfake technology, another application of generative AI, serves as a powerful illustration of how AI can manipulate and create realistic simulations of audio and video content. Deepfakes use a form of machine learning known as generative adversarial networks (GANs), which pit two neural networks against each other to produce increasingly convincing fake content. This technology is capable of altering video footage so that individuals appear to say or do things they never did. It has profound implications, from enhancing entertainment experiences to raising ethical concerns about misinformation. For instance, filmmakers can resurrect historical figures or bring fictional characters to life with uncanny realism.

By examining these applications, one can begin to demystify the concept of generative AI. Often perceived as complex and abstract, generative AI becomes more tangible through the concrete outputs it produces, such as artwork and videos. This demystification is crucial, especially for beginners and professionals seeking to grasp AI's potential. By understanding these examples, individuals can better appreciate how generative AI operates and what it can achieve.

Moreover, AI-generated artwork and deepfakes highlight generative AI's significant role in fostering originality across various creative domains. In music, for example, AI can compose original scores that blend different genres, generating fresh musical experiences. Artists and musicians now collaborate with AI, exploring creative synergies that push boundaries and expand their repertoires. Similarly, writers use AI tools to craft new narratives, assisted by algorithms that suggest plot twists and character developments.

Through these innovations, readers gain insights into how generative AI continuously extends the horizons of creativity and innovation. In the fashion industry, designers leverage AI to propose novel garment designs rapidly, experimenting with fabric patterns and color combinations that might be challenging to conceive manually. In architecture, generative algorithms help architects explore unconventional building forms and optimize designs for sustainability and efficiency.

Furthermore, generative AI showcases its capacity to expand innovation across numerous sectors beyond the arts. In advertising, AI-generated campaigns demonstrate creativity by customizing content for diverse audiences, enhancing engagement through tailored visuals and messages. In manufacturing, generative design software enables engineers to develop high-performance parts with optimized structures, reducing material usage while maintaining strength—a key advantage in creating more sustainable products.

Education is yet another field benefiting from generative AI's broadening scope. Educators incorporate AI tools to create interactive learning materials that adapt to students' progress and interests. AI-generated exercises and simulations provide immersive experiences, making complex subjects more accessible and engaging to learners of all ages.

The interplay between generative AI and innovation also manifests in the development of smart cities. Urban planners utilize AI-driven models to simulate infrastructure changes, optimizing traffic flows and energy consumption. This forward-thinking approach fosters efficient resource management, contributing to sustainable urban development.

Understanding these diverse applications helps illustrate how generative AI continues to redefine norms and drive progress across sectors. As technology evolves, professionals and educators must stay informed to leverage these advancements effectively. By embracing generative AI, industries can unlock new potentials, fostering environments that nurture creativity and adaptive thinking.

CHAPTER 5

AI Tools and Platforms for Beginners

Exploring AI tools and platforms is essential for anyone beginning their journey into artificial intelligence. With the rapid growth and influence of AI technology in various fields, having a foundational understanding of these tools is invaluable. For novices, these resources are designed to simplify complex processes, making the initial steps less daunting and more engaging. The accessibility and functionality of these platforms not only demystify AI but also inspire confidence in users, allowing them to experiment without fear of overwhelming technical difficulties. As you navigate through this chapter, you will discover how choosing the right platform can align with your learning goals, personal interests, and professional aspirations, setting the stage for effective development and application of AI skills.

This chapter will introduce several key AI tools and platforms tailored specifically for beginners eager to delve into AI development. You will encounter a variety of options that cater to different needs, from those that offer powerful computational capabilities without cost to others that provide intuitive, no-code environments ideal for educators and students. Additionally, the chapter will highlight platforms that encourage collaborative and experiential learning, such as online communities where you can practice with real-world datasets and interact with other AI practitioners. By providing an overview of these diverse resources, the chapter aims to equip you with the knowledge needed to confidently begin your AI journey, understand their unique advantages, and select those that best support your current level of expertise and future learning objectives.

Popular AI Development Platforms

In today's fast-paced world of technology, understanding and utilizing AI tools is crucial not only for those embarking on a new career path but also for established professionals seeking to enhance their skill set. For beginners interested in AI development, several accessible platforms can facilitate your learning journey and provide the resources needed to start building AI projects. These tools vary widely in their offerings but share the common goal of making AI approachable and manageable, even for those with minimal experience.

Google Colab stands out as an excellent starting point for novice AI enthusiasts. Its appeal lies in its user-friendly environment that requires no installations, as it operates entirely through a web browser. What makes Google Colab particularly attractive is its provision of free GPU support, which is instrumental in handling complex computations efficiently. This capability is invaluable for training and testing models, where speed and processing power are essential. Additionally, the seamless integration with Google Drive allows for straightforward data management, enabling users to store datasets and projects in a centralized location. This feature simplifies the workflow and provides easy access to files from any device, thereby enhancing collaboration and flexibility.

Microsoft Azure Machine Learning offers another robust platform for AI beginners, especially those without coding expertise. Boasting a no-code interface, Microsoft Azure enables users to build machine learning models through a simple drag-and-drop visual environment. This aspect makes it particularly appealing for educators and students who may want to focus more on understanding concepts rather than coding specifics. Furthermore, Microsoft Azure extends comprehensive tutorials that guide users step-by-step through various processes, ensuring a smooth learning curve. The platform also emphasizes team collaboration features, allowing multiple users to work concurrently on the same project—a valuable asset for educational settings or professional teams aiming to integrate machine learning into their operations without extensive programming knowledge.

Another significant player in the realm of AI development is IBM Watson Studio. This platform appeals to users keen on exploring a variety of programming environments, offering support for multiple languages like Python, R, and Scala. IBM Watson Studio's strength lies in its ability to simplify model building through a visual interface, providing tools that allow users to design, train, and deploy machine learning models with ease. Much like its peers, it champions collaboration by facilitating shared project spaces where team members can collectively contribute to machine learning initiatives. This setup promotes a unified approach to problem-solving, which is crucial in both academic and business contexts. By incorporating diverse functionalities and a collaborative framework, IBM Watson Studio positions itself as an ideal tool for users looking to delve deeper into AI applications while benefitting from a structured, supportive environment.

For individuals who thrive on community engagement and hands-on learning, Kaggle serves as an indispensable resource. As a well-known online platform dedicated to data science and machine learning, Kaggle offers a wealth of datasets contributed by a global community of practitioners and researchers. These datasets are pivotal for learners wishing to practice their skills on real-world data, moving beyond theoretical exercises. Additionally, Kaggle hosts numerous community-shared code notebooks, which are essentially detailed walkthroughs of various data science problems and solutions. These notebooks act as educational guides, illustrating how experienced users tackle data challenges, thus serving as a rich source of insight for beginners. Kaggle also fosters networking within the data science community, providing forums and discussion boards where users can connect, discuss techniques, and collaborate on projects. Engaging with this community can be incredibly beneficial for learners to gather feedback, learn best practices, and stay updated on the latest industry trends.

Each platform discussed here presents unique advantages tailored to different aspects of AI development. Google Colab is perfect for those seeking a straightforward entry point with powerful computational capabilities at no cost. In contrast, Microsoft Azure Machine Learning provides a no-code solution with a focus on collaborative, real-world applications, making it suitable for beginners who prefer a more guided approach. IBM Watson Studio, with its multi-language support and collaborative tools, accommodates those looking to explore diverse programming options and engage in teamwork-oriented projects. Meanwhile, Kaggle stands out as a hub for practical learning and community involvement, encouraging users to deepen their understanding through real-world data and peer interaction.

Resources for Learning and Practicing AI

When you are just starting out in the field of artificial intelligence (AI), it can feel overwhelming due to the vast amount of information and resources available. However, there are several learning pathways that can simplify this journey. An excellent place to begin is with online education platforms such as Coursera and edX. These websites offer a plethora of courses designed by esteemed universities across the globe. What makes these courses particularly accessible is their flexibility in payment options, offering free classes or financial aid for those who need it. Many of these courses have a project-based structure. This means you aren't just passively consuming information; instead, you're applying what you've learned in real-world scenarios, significantly enhancing your understanding. The involvement of university instructors ensures that you receive high-quality education and guidance throughout your learning process.

The visual nature of AI concepts often requires more than just reading text or looking at static images. Here's where YouTube steps in as a powerful educational tool. Channels like 3Blue1Brown and Sentdex are worth exploring as they use videos to unpack complex AI ideas through informal, interactive storytelling and demonstrations. These channels have a knack for transforming challenging topics into digestible pieces, making them comprehensible even to beginners without extensive prior knowledge. Additionally, because these creators regularly upload content, you are constantly updated on the latest trends and breakthroughs in AI. This dynamic form of learning ensures you are not only keeping pace with current advancements but also engaging with the material in an enjoyable way.

Books remain invaluable, particularly when they delve deeply into subjects like AI and machine learning. One noteworthy title is "Hands-On Machine Learning with Scikit-Learn, Keras, and TensorFlow." This book serves multiple functions: it acts as a comprehensive guide, a practical workbook, and a reference manual. With its focused approach on practical application rather than theoretical abstraction, readers gain hands-on experience through exercises that cement their understanding. It provides detailed insights into how to implement algorithms using popular tools and frameworks, which is essential for building a robust foundation in AI and machine learning. Over time, this book can become a go-to resource, reinforcing concepts long after you have completed your initial read-through.

Interacting with peers and industry professionals adds another layer to one's learning experience. AI community forums, such as Reddit's r/MachineLearning, are vibrant hubs of discussion and information sharing. Here, learning goes beyond textbooks and lectures to include real-world insights from those already working in the field. Engaging with these communities gives you access to diverse perspectives and solutions to common problems. Networking within these forums can open up opportunities for collaboration on projects, sharing experiences that might not be captured within formal education. By participating actively, users benefit from peer support which often boosts motivation and keeps engagement levels high. For educators and students, these forums can serve as supplementary sources of material and inspiration, helping integrate contemporary AI discussions into academic settings.

Beginner-Friendly Programming Languages for AI

For those venturing into the realm of Artificial Intelligence (AI), selecting the right programming language is a critical first step. This subpoint will unravel various programming languages that are particularly accessible and practical for beginners in AI development.

Python stands out as a preferred choice among budding AI developers. Its simplicity and readability make it an approachable option for those new to programming, allowing learners to focus more on learning AI concepts rather than grappling with complex syntax. Python's popularity is further cemented by its robust community support, which means there's a wealth of tutorials, forums, and documentation available. Of significant importance are the extensive libraries tailored for AI and machine learning, such as TensorFlow and PyTorch. These libraries simplify many aspects of AI development by providing pre-built functions and models, enabling beginners to implement AI solutions without starting from scratch. For instance, TensorFlow's Keras API allows users to prototype deep learning models quickly, making it easier to experiment and iterate. PyTorch, with its dynamic computational graph, offers flexibility and ease in debugging, which are great assets for those still finding their footing. Hence, Python's blend of readability and powerful tools makes it ideal for beginners eager to dive into AI.

R is another language worthy of consideration, especially for those interested in statistical analysis and data visualization. Renowned for its prowess in handling statistical data, R provides an array of packages designed for AI applications, such as caret and mlr3. These packages facilitate tasks ranging from basic data manipulation to complex predictive modeling. R excels in situations requiring detailed statistical insights, making it a strong candidate for projects involving substantial data analytics. Its rich graphical capabilities also make it suitable for creating detailed visualizations, an essential feature when analyzing and interpreting complex data sets. For example, R's ggplot2 library offers a versatile framework for crafting detailed plots, helping convey findings in an accessible manner. Consequently, R's statistical strengths and visualization tools can significantly benefit AI practitioners whose work involves in-depth data analysis.

JavaScript might not be the first language that comes to mind when thinking about AI, but it holds a unique position in the sphere of web-based applications. As web technologies continue to advance, embedding AI directly into web interfaces becomes increasingly relevant. JavaScript, through frameworks like TensorFlow.js, allows developers to run machine learning models directly in the browser. This capability opens up avenues for real-time data processing and user interaction enhancements within web applications. The advantage of using JavaScript for AI lies in its seamless integration with front-end development, enabling developers to embed AI functionalities into interactive web user interfaces effortlessly. For example, creating a website capable of facial recognition or speech processing becomes feasible without needing server-side computations, thanks to JavaScript's ability to handle these tasks client-side. This makes JavaScript a compelling choice for developers focusing on user-centric AI features within web environments.

Julia is an emerging language that combines the ease of Python with the performance of C++, offering a unique platform for high-performance computing. Julia is designed to fill the gap where computational speed meets developer productivity, making it ideal for prototyping AI solutions that require significant computational power. Its syntax is clean and intuitive, similar to Python, which reduces the learning curve for beginners. Yet, Julia's standout feature is its execution speed, which can be crucial for data-heavy AI tasks or simulations. Libraries like Flux.jl provide users with tools to build machine learning models efficiently, leveraging Julia's speed. This is particularly useful in domains requiring large-scale computations, such as neural networks or complex simulations. With the ability to quickly iterate and test models due to its fast execution, Julia empowers both newcomers and experienced developers to explore AI possibilities extensively.

Setting Up Your First AI Environment

Starting an AI journey can be both thrilling and intimidating for beginners. One of the first practical steps to dive into AI development is setting up a fundamental coding environment that aligns with your needs and aspirations. Choosing the right Integrated Development Environment (IDE) is crucial, as it directly impacts how you interact with your code.

For many novices, Jupyter Notebook stands out due to its interactive nature. It allows users to write and test segments of code in individual cells, making it easy to iteratively develop ideas and immediately visualize results. This interactivity is especially beneficial when learning data analysis or experimenting with machine learning models, as you can see the effect of changes instantly and make real-time adjustments.

On the other hand, PyCharm offers a more comprehensive set of tools aimed at larger programming projects. What makes PyCharm appealing is its robust debugging tools, which are essential when you're diving deeper into complex algorithms and need to understand why a piece of code isn't functioning as expected. While it may have a steeper learning curve than Jupyter Notebooks, PyCharm's features can become crucial assets as projects grow in scale and intricacy.

Once you've settled on an IDE, the next step is to install key libraries that form the backbone of many AI projects. Libraries like NumPy, pandas, and scikit-learn are indispensable in this regard. NumPy provides support for large multidimensional arrays and matrices, along with a collection of mathematical functions to operate on these structures. Pandas offers data structures and tools needed for effective data manipulation and analysis, providing intuitive ways to handle data through series and DataFrames.

Scikit-learn, meanwhile, is tailored specifically for machine learning. It includes simple and efficient tools for data mining, data analysis, and supporting a range of supervised and unsupervised learning algorithms. The installation process for these libraries typically involves using pip, the Python package manager, via command-line instructions like pip install numpy, ensuring they're accessible in your coding environment.

Understanding how to access datasets is another fundamental skill to master. Platforms such as Kaggle offer a treasure trove of data across various domains, from healthcare to financial analytics. Sourcing data from Kaggle not only exposes you to diverse scenarios and datasets but also helps bridge the gap between theoretical knowledge and practical application. Engaging with real-world data requires cleaning and preprocessing it before any meaningful analysis can occur, introducing vital data cleaning processes. This experience enriches your comprehension of how data shapes models and outcomes.

Furthermore, running simple AI code demonstrations is perhaps one of the most enlightening exercises you can undertake. By integrating theory with hands-on experiments, you solidify your understanding of basic concepts and build a foundation that supports more advanced learning. Starting with simple algorithms, such as linear regression or k-nearest neighbors, allows you to dissect each step of model building—from importing libraries and loading datasets to training the model and evaluating its performance. Doing so not only boosts your confidence but also establishes a concrete workflow comprehension, guiding you from initial coding to proficient execution.

Embarking on an AI journey requires patience and persistence. By initially focusing on creating a comfortable and efficient coding setup, you build a strong launching pad for future explorations. Selecting between Jupyter Notebook and PyCharm depends largely on your immediate goals and desired workflow. Installing key libraries like NumPy, pandas, and scikit-learn equips you with essential tools for undertaking data-related tasks.

Leveraging Collaboration and Networking in AI

In the rapidly evolving landscape of artificial intelligence (AI), the importance of collaborative learning and networking cannot be overstated. These elements are critical in enhancing one's proficiency and ensuring effective skill development within this complex field. For beginners, as well as those seeking to expand their expertise, leveraging collaborative platforms and engaging in networking opportunities can significantly accelerate learning and application of AI concepts.

Collaborative platforms are transformative tools that enable shared learning experiences by fostering teamwork, knowledge exchange, and idea sharing. These platforms leverage cloud services, allowing for the execution of joint AI projects, which are invaluable for novices eager to understand real-world applications. Google Colab, for instance, facilitates such collaboration by offering a shared workspace where users can work on Python notebooks simultaneously, integrating seamlessly with Google Drive for data storage and management. This not only reduces the need for high-end hardware but also promotes a culture of collective problem-solving where team members can contribute diverse skills and perspectives toward project completion.

Engaging with AI communities through networking opportunities propels learners into environments ripe with innovation and creativity. Participating in competitions like Kaggle or conferences such as NeurIPS allows individuals to connect with fellow enthusiasts, researchers, and professionals. These interactions are instrumental in exposing learners to cutting-edge developments and varied methodologies within the AI field. Networking provides a platform for exchanging insights on best practices, innovative techniques, and emerging trends, significantly enriching the learning experience. It opens doors to mentorship, which is particularly beneficial for beginners who may struggle to navigate the complexities of AI alone.

The participation in online forums further expands one's learning horizon by inviting dialogue and debate among diverse groups. Platforms like Stack Overflow or Reddit's r/MachineLearning become crucibles for exchanging ideas and solutions to complex AI challenges. Engaging with these communities exposes participants to a multitude of perspectives, encouraging them to consider alternative approaches to problem-solving. This exposure fosters a comprehensive understanding of AI principles by highlighting different ways to address similar problems, ultimately leading to the development of more robust and versatile problem-solving strategies.

Continuous feedback from peers and experts is another integral component of collaborative learning that supports the journey toward AI mastery. Regular interaction with experienced practitioners offers constructive criticism, helping learners identify areas that require improvement while simultaneously affirming their strengths. This form of iterative learning encourages adaptation and refinement of skills, enabling learners to tailor their educational journey according to their individual progress and goals. Feedback loops nurture an environment of support and motivation, crucial for overcoming the inevitable challenges encountered in the AI field.

These collaborative efforts are especially relevant for educators aiming to incorporate AI into their curricula. By engaging students in collaborative learning and networking, educators can offer practical experiences that emphasize teamwork, critical thinking, and the application of theoretical knowledge in real-world scenarios. As students interact with peers and professionals, they gain insights into the ethical implications and societal impacts of AI technologies, preparing them to think critically about the role AI plays in various fields.

Students pursuing careers in STEM fields stand to benefit immensely from these collaborative and networking experiences. Engaging in team-based AI projects and participating in AI-focused communities can enhance their academic experience, providing them with practical skills and improving their employability. Through these interactions, students learn to apply classroom knowledge to tangible problems, bridging the gap between theory and practice. This hands-on learning approach is essential for developing a holistic understanding of AI technologies and their vast applications across industries.

For professionals looking to stay competitive in today's technology-driven job market, networking and collaboration serve as avenues for continuous learning and skill enhancement. As they engage with AI communities, professionals can stay abreast of technological advancements and industry standards, ensuring their skills remain relevant and up-to-date. Collaborative projects allow these individuals to experiment with new tools and methodologies, fostering innovation and adaptability in their work processes.

CHAPTER 6

Practical Applications of AI

Artificial Intelligence (AI) is reshaping various facets of human life, playing a crucial role in diverse fields from healthcare to business operations. Its transformative power lies in its ability to automate processes, analyze massive datasets, and produce actionable insights. AI doesn't merely replicate human intelligence but enhances decision-making and efficiency across sectors, making it an invaluable asset for both beginners eager to understand new technologies and seasoned professionals seeking to refine their expertise. As AI becomes more integrated into our daily routines, understanding its applications and benefits has become essential for anyone looking to stay competitive in today's technology-driven world.

In this chapter, the focus will be on exploring the practical real-world applications of AI. We will delve into how AI revolutionizes healthcare by improving diagnostics and personalizing treatment plans, providing critical support in patient care. The discussion will extend to the impact of AI on business operations, highlighting advancements in predictive analytics, customer service, and task automation that drive organizational success. Further exploration will cover AI's influence in education, where personalized learning experiences and automated assessments redefine student engagement and teacher productivity. Additionally, we'll examine how AI integrates seamlessly into consumer products, enhancing convenience through smart home devices and personalized shopping recommendations. By illustrating these applications, the chapter aims to provide readers with a comprehensive understanding of AI's transformative effects and its potential to optimize various aspects of industry and everyday life.

AI in Healthcare: Diagnostics and Treatment Plans

Artificial Intelligence (AI) is ushering in a new era in healthcare, revolutionizing diagnostics and tailoring treatment plans with unprecedented precision. One of the most significant contributions of AI in this field is its ability to analyze medical images for early disease detection. Advanced algorithms can scrutinize X-rays, MRIs, and CT scans at a speed and accuracy that often surpass human capabilities. This technology not only accelerates the diagnostic process but also enhances the early detection of diseases like cancer, where identifying abnormalities in the initial stages is critical for successful treatment outcomes. For instance, studies have illustrated how AI systems successfully detect early-stage lung cancer nodules with higher accuracy than conventional radiologists, providing a life-saving advantage in patient care.

Moreover, AI's capabilities extend beyond imaging to include predictive analytics for patient outcomes. Machine learning algorithms play a pivotal role in evaluating vast datasets to forecast the trajectory of a patient's health. By analyzing factors such as medical history, lab results, and genetic information, these algorithms can identify patients at high risk of developing specific conditions. For example, AI has been used to predict the likelihood of cardiovascular events by analyzing patterns in patient data, allowing healthcare providers to implement preventative measures proactively. Such insights enable practitioners to develop personalized preventive strategies, ultimately reducing the incidence of severe health episodes and improving patient quality of life.

Delving deeper into personalization, AI is instrumental in crafting individualized treatment plans based on a patient's unique genetic makeup. This approach, often referred to as precision medicine, allows for treatments that are specifically tailored to suit individual genetic profiles, thereby optimizing the efficacy of interventions. In oncology, for instance, AI analyzes genetic mutations within tumors to recommend precise chemotherapy regimens, significantly boosting success rates compared to traditional trial-and-error methods. Patients receive therapies that target specific biological pathways associated with their condition, minimizing adverse effects and enhancing recovery prospects.

AI-powered virtual health assistants represent another transformative application. These digital tools provide round-the-clock support, helping patients manage chronic conditions like diabetes or hypertension. They offer medication reminders, monitor vital signs, and even suggest lifestyle adjustments, thereby promoting adherence to treatment plans. In emergency situations, virtual assistants can perform preliminary assessments, helping users determine the severity of symptoms and advising on the need for immediate medical attention. By increasing accessibility and engagement, these applications empower patients to actively participate in their healthcare journey, fostering better health outcomes.

In addition to individual benefits, AI's integration into healthcare leads to systemic improvements. The ability of AI to manage and interpret large volumes of data facilitates enhanced operational efficiency across healthcare facilities. Automated processes streamline administrative tasks, freeing up medical professionals to focus on patient care. Furthermore, AI-driven insights guide resource allocation, ensuring that hospitals utilize their personnel and facilities optimally, thus reducing costs and enhancing service delivery.

Transforming Business Operations with AI

In today's fast-paced business environment, leveraging technology for better decision-making is crucial, and artificial intelligence (AI) plays a pivotal role in optimizing these processes. One of the standout applications is predictive analytics powered by AI, which allows businesses to anticipate market trends effectively. By analyzing vast datasets, AI identifies patterns that might be invisible to human analysts, providing insights into future market behaviors. For instance, a retail company can use AI models to predict seasonal demand spikes, enabling it to adjust its inventory accordingly. This level of anticipation allows businesses to craft proactive strategies, stay ahead of competitors, and respond swiftly to changing market dynamics.

Another significant application of AI in business is through chatbots. These AI-driven systems revolutionize customer service by offering 24/7 support, addressing customer inquiries with speed and efficiency. Unlike traditional customer service setups that rely heavily on human agents and are limited by working hours, AI chatbots can handle numerous queries simultaneously, reducing wait times and enhancing the overall customer experience. For example, in the banking sector, chatbots can assist users with transactions, account management, and provide instant solutions to frequently asked questions. The continuous availability and rapid response nature of chatbots not only improve customer satisfaction but also bolster brand loyalty, as clients appreciate the seamless interaction.

Moreover, AI significantly affects routine task automation, proving to be a game-changer for organizational productivity. Repetitive tasks like data entry, scheduling, and report generation can be automated using AI technologies, relieving employees from mundane duties. This shift allows the workforce to focus on more strategic and creative initiatives that drive innovation and growth. In a typical office setting, for example, software that automatically inputs invoice details or schedules meetings frees up time for staff to engage in higher-level problem-solving activities or strategic planning sessions. This transformation not only enhances productivity but also boosts employee morale, as individuals feel empowered to contribute to meaningful projects rather than being bogged down by repetitive tasks.

Supply chain management stands as another domain where AI's influence is profoundly felt. The complexity of supply chains necessitates advanced tools for efficient management, and AI fits this role perfectly by optimizing inventory needs and improving logistics planning. Through machine learning algorithms and real-time data analysis, AI systems can forecast inventory requirements, ensuring that companies maintain optimal stock levels without overstocking or facing shortages. Logistics becomes smoother as AI predicts potential disruptions and suggests alternative routes or methods of transportation. Companies in sectors like manufacturing and retail benefit immensely from such optimizations; reduced operational costs and improved delivery speeds lead to enhanced customer satisfaction and strengthen business relationships.

Impact of AI on Education and Training

Artificial Intelligence (AI) has revolutionized numerous fields, and education is no exception. One of the main contributions AI offers is personalized learning experiences. Traditionally, educators have faced the challenge of catering to diverse learning styles within a single classroom. The advent of AI has alleviated this issue by enabling customized learning paths. By analyzing data related to student performance and preferences, AI algorithms can identify individual strengths and weaknesses. Consequently, they provide tailored educational resources such as exercises and readings that align with each student's unique needs.

For instance, a student who struggles with abstract concepts might benefit from visual aids provided through AI tools, whereas another who excels in verbal reasoning might receive challenging text-based problems. This customization not only bolsters engagement but also fosters a deeper understanding of the subject matter. As students are presented with content that resonates with them personally, their motivation to learn increases, leading to improved academic outcomes.

Beyond personalization, AI-driven assessment tools play a critical role in modern education. These tools offer instant feedback on quizzes and assignments, allowing educators to rapidly gauge student comprehension. Such immediate insights enable teachers to modify their instructional strategies promptly. For example, if a significant number of students perform poorly on a specific topic, an instructor can revisit the material, employing alternative teaching methods to enhance clarity. This adaptability ensures that educators can address learning gaps more efficiently than ever before, promoting a supportive learning environment where students are less likely to fall behind.

Moreover, AI's capability to automate administrative tasks significantly boosts teacher productivity. Activities like grading, attendance tracking, and report generation, which traditionally consume a considerable amount of time, can now be streamlined through AI applications. By delegating these routine responsibilities to AI, educators can reallocate their time and energy towards innovative lesson planning and creating enriching classroom experiences. This shift not only enriches the educational process but also empowers teachers to focus on fostering critical thinking and creativity among their students.

Interactive technologies, powered by AI, further revolutionize the learning experience. Tools such as virtual reality (VR) create immersive learning environments that actively engage students, leading to better retention and understanding of complex subjects. For instance, in a history class, students can virtually explore ancient civilizations, walking through reconstructed sites and experiencing historical events firsthand. Such experiences make learning vivid and memorable, bridging the gap between theoretical knowledge and practical application.

The use of VR in science education provides another compelling example. Students can conduct virtual experiments in a risk-free setting, observing chemical reactions that are too dangerous or impractical for a traditional classroom. This hands-on approach enhances comprehension and facilitates experiential learning, which is crucial for grasping intricate scientific principles. By simulating real-world scenarios, AI-driven interactive technologies prepare students for future challenges in their respective fields.

Instructors, too, benefit from these advancements. With access to AI-generated analytics, they gain insights into student engagement levels during virtual sessions. This information can guide instructors in customizing their approaches, ensuring that interactive elements are optimally integrated into lessons. Through continuous refinement of their teaching methods, educators can cultivate an atmosphere that encourages active participation and sustained interest in learning.

Furthermore, AI's influence extends beyond individual classrooms, impacting educational institutions on a broader scale. Schools adopting AI technology often witness enhanced overall efficiency. Streamlined administrative processes contribute to a seamless educational ecosystem where resources are allocated effectively, and operational hurdles are minimized. Moreover, by facilitating communication between various stakeholders—teachers, students, and parents—AI fosters collaboration and transparency, ultimately benefiting the entire school community.

AI in Everyday Consumer Products

Artificial Intelligence (AI) has become an integral part of our daily lives, seamlessly integrating into various aspects of modern living to enhance convenience and personalization. One prominent example is smart home devices, which have revolutionized how we interact with our living spaces. Devices such as smart thermostats, lights, and security cameras adapt to user preferences by learning patterns and routines. For instance, a smart thermostat can learn when you typically leave for work and return home, adjusting temperatures accordingly to ensure comfort while maximizing energy efficiency. These devices also incorporate safety enhancements: smart locks and doorbells monitor entry points and alert homeowners of unusual activity, adding an extra layer of security.

In the realm of ecommerce, AI plays a crucial role in providing personalized recommendations, transforming consumer shopping experiences. Online platforms like Amazon and Netflix employ sophisticated algorithms to analyze past purchase history, browsing behavior, and ratings to suggest products or content tailored to individual tastes. By presenting users with options that align closely with their preferences, these systems not only boost sales conversions but also enhance customer satisfaction through curated shopping experiences. This personalization extends beyond product recommendations; AI-powered virtual assistants, such as chatbots, provide immediate responses to inquiries, further enriching the shopping journey by offering assistance and support.

Wearable fitness trackers are another manifestation of AI's integration into everyday life, offering personalized health insights to users. Devices such as Fitbit and Apple Watch monitor physical activity, heart rate, sleep patterns, and more, providing users with detailed analyses of their health data. AI algorithms process this information to deliver customized feedback and suggestions, encouraging users to make informed decisions about their lifestyle choices. For instance, if a tracker detects insufficient sleep over several nights, it might suggest earlier bedtimes or relaxation techniques. These wearable devices empower individuals to manage their health proactively, offering reminders and motivational prompts to maintain fitness goals.

The field of automated content creation has also benefited substantially from AI innovations, particularly in marketing and communication. AI-driven tools generate personalized marketing materials efficiently, allowing businesses to adapt and customize content to suit diverse audiences. From email campaigns to social media posts, AI analyzes audience interactions and data to produce engaging content that resonates with its target demographic. This approach not only cuts costs related to manual content creation but also speeds up delivery times, ensuring timely dissemination of marketing messages. The ability to tailor content dynamically means that businesses can reach consumers more effectively, reinforcing brand loyalty and fostering customer engagement.

As AI continues to evolve, its impact on daily life grows increasingly profound, reshaping how we perform routine tasks and interact with technology. These advancements not only increase convenience but also offer unprecedented levels of personalization, catering to individual needs and preferences. Whether adjusting the ambiance of a home, enhancing shopping experiences, promoting healthier lifestyles, or streamlining marketing processes, AI demonstrates its potential to enrich and simplify everyday experiences.

One notable example of AI's influence is seen in the way people manage their homes with voice-activated assistants like Amazon Alexa and Google Assistant. These devices allow users to control home environments using simple voice commands, facilitating hands-free operation of appliances, entertainment systems, and more. As they become more intuitive, these assistants provide a seamless interface between humans and technology, anticipating needs and responding appropriately without requiring direct input. By learning from user interactions, they refine their responses and capabilities, further enhancing user experience.

Similarly, the retail landscape has been transformed by AI's capacity to interpret vast amounts of consumer data to predict trends and preferences. Retailers leverage this technology to strategically position products, optimize inventory, and even design store layouts based on predictive models. This data-driven approach minimizes wastage and ensures that popular items are readily available, meeting consumer demand more accurately. Such strategic planning reflects AI's ability to optimize operations while simultaneously improving customer satisfaction.

Moreover, in the realm of personal health management, wearable devices utilizing AI now offer insights beyond fitness tracking. They are beginning to integrate features that detect irregularities in vital signs, potentially alerting users to health issues before they become significant concerns. By empowering individuals with actionable information, AI fosters a more proactive approach to health care, encouraging preventive measures and timely medical consultation.

Beyond immediate consumer applications, the efficiency brought forth by AI automation extends to digital marketing realms where AI-generated content adapts based on user engagement metrics. Marketers can leverage AI tools to conduct A/B tests, evaluate campaign effectiveness, and fine-tune strategies in real-time, maximizing outreach and minimizing resource expenditure. In essence, the power of AI in content creation lies in its adaptability and scalability, enabling content producers to respond swiftly to audience needs and preferences.

As these technologies continue to develop, the landscape of AI application in daily life will undoubtedly expand further. Future innovations may introduce even more sophisticated mechanisms for personalizing user experiences, tailoring services to fit unique individual demands with precision and efficiency. In doing so, AI promises to redefine the boundaries of what's possible, guiding us into an era where technology instinctively understands and responds to human needs.

AI's Contribution to Societal Advancements

Artificial intelligence (AI) has a profound societal impact with immense potential to address some of the world's most pressing global challenges. One significant area where AI is making strides is in environmental monitoring. By analyzing vast datasets, AI can track climate change patterns and biodiversity loss. These technologies are adept at processing signals from satellites and ground-based sensors, leading to improved understanding and real-time updating on environmental conditions. For instance, machine learning algorithms sift through copious amounts of data to identify patterns that might go undetected by human observers. This capability enhances our ability to predict changes in weather systems, understand the dynamics of ecosystems, and better manage conservation efforts. Consequently, scientists and policymakers armed with this information can develop more effective strategies for combating climate change and protecting endangered species.

In addition to environmental monitoring, AI plays a crucial role in disaster response. Traditionally, predicting natural disasters has been fraught with uncertainty; however, AI's predictive analytics offer a beacon of hope. By employing machine learning models that analyze seismic, meteorological, and other environmental data, AI provides early warnings about possible natural disasters like earthquakes, hurricanes, and floods. For example, during hurricane season, AI algorithms can process satellite images and atmospheric data much faster than traditional methods, delivering crucial updates that can save lives. Such timely alerts allow communities to prepare adequately, minimizing damage and potentially saving lives. Governments and aid organizations can make informed decisions regarding resource allocation and evacuation strategies, thereby enhancing overall preparedness and resilience against natural calamities.

Furthermore, the influence of AI extends into scientific research, particularly in areas such as genomics and drug discovery. The complexity of biological data often presents formidable challenges to researchers. Here, AI excels by processing intricate datasets, uncovering relationships, and patterns that may not be immediately apparent through conventional means. In genomics, AI tools facilitate the analysis of genetic sequences, speeding up discoveries related to disease markers and genetic variations. This approach enables researchers to develop personalized medicine strategies tailored to individual genetic profiles, promising improved treatment outcomes.

Similarly, AI-driven techniques revolutionize the field of drug discovery. Traditionally, developing new pharmaceuticals is a lengthy and costly endeavor involving thousands of compounds and extensive testing. AI significantly shortens this timeline by efficiently sifting through chemical databases and simulating interactions between drugs and target proteins. By identifying promising candidates faster, pharmaceutical companies can accelerate the development of life-saving medications, bringing them to market more swiftly and cost-effectively. The synergy between AI and research breakthroughs continues to broaden the horizon of human knowledge, driving forward fields that impact every facet of society.

Moreover, AI is transforming agriculture through precision farming practices. In the quest for sustainable agriculture, AI offers innovative solutions to optimize resource use and improve crop yields. Precision farming leverages AI technology to monitor soil conditions, water levels, and crop health, enabling farmers to make data-driven decisions. Drones equipped with AI-powered imaging systems can survey large tracts of farmland, identifying areas that require attention. These insights help farmers apply fertilizers, pesticides, and water precisely where needed, reducing waste and increasing efficiency.

Additionally, AI tools analyze weather patterns, offering recommendations on the best times for planting or harvesting crops, further boosting productivity. This level of optimization ensures that agricultural practices are both economically viable and environmentally sustainable, providing a blueprint for feeding the world's growing population while minimizing ecological impact. As we advance deeper into the digital age, the integration of AI in agriculture not only supports food security but also paves the way for more innovative farming strategies that prioritize sustainability.

CHAPTER 7

Hands-On AI Exercises

ngaging with hands-on AI exercises bridges the gap between theoretical knowledge and practical application. In the realm of artificial intelligence, experiential learning allows both beginners and seasoned professionals to gain a deeper understanding by actively participating in the creation and implementation of AI models. Such exercises foster an environment where experimentation leads to innovation. This approach not only solidifies foundational concepts but also enhances problem-solving skills by offering real-world scenarios where these techniques can be applied directly. For educators seeking to incorporate AI into their curriculum, hands-on exercises provide a compelling means to demonstrate AI's relevance and power, making the subject matter more accessible and engaging for students.

The chapter delves into constructing a simple classification model, guiding readers through each step from selecting appropriate datasets to evaluating model performance. It provides practical advice on choosing machine learning algorithms, such as logistic regression and decision trees, and highlights essential processes like data preprocessing and test-train splitting. Techniques for enhancing model efficiency and accuracy are explored, fostering an iterative development mindset. Readers will learn how to apply these skills in various contexts, such as spam detection or customer sentiment analysis, solidifying their understanding through relevant examples. By the end of this chapter, you will have acquired valuable skills to build effective AI solutions across different industries.

Building a Simple Classification Model

Classification is a foundational concept in artificial intelligence, serving as a powerful tool for categorizing data into distinct groups. This process is integral to various applications, as it allows us to make sense of vast datasets by organizing them into recognizable patterns or classes. The primary objective of classification is to predict the category to which a new observation belongs based on its features. Understanding this objective is crucial, as it lays the groundwork for numerous practical applications that impact our daily lives and work environments.

One compelling real-world example illustrating the importance of classification is spam detection in email systems. Classification models are employed to automatically sort incoming emails into categories like "spam" or "not spam," enhancing user experience by saving time and improving security. This process involves analyzing email content, sender details, and historical data to determine whether an email should be considered spam. Such practical benefits demonstrate classification's significance in automating decision-making processes across various industries.

Creating a basic classification model is approachable with accessible tools and a structured approach. Let's explore a step-by-step guide to developing your first classification model. Start by selecting a dataset relevant to your interests or needs. Websites like Kaggle and UCI Machine Learning Repository host a variety of datasets suitable for beginners. Once you have chosen a dataset, the next step is data preprocessing, involving cleaning and preparing the data for analysis.

Data preprocessing includes handling missing values, transforming categorical data into numerical format, and normalizing features to ensure they contribute equally to the model. After preprocessing, it's essential to split the data into training and testing sets, typically using a ratio such as 80/20. This split ensures that the model can learn from one subset and validate its accuracy on another.

With prepared data, choose a machine learning algorithm suitable for classification tasks. Common algorithms include logistic regression, decision trees, and support vector machines, among others. For beginners, starting with a simple algorithm like logistic regression can provide valuable insights into the workings of classification without overwhelming complexity. Many popular programming languages, including Python, offer libraries such as Scikit-learn, which simplify the implementation of these algorithms.

Implementing the chosen algorithm involves fitting the model to the training data. This process entails feeding the algorithm with feature data and corresponding labels so that it learns the relationship between input features and their associated class labels. Once fitted, the model can predict the classifications of new, unseen data.

Testing the model's performance is crucial to ensure its reliability. Evaluating a classification model involves calculating metrics like accuracy, precision, recall, and F1-score. Accuracy measures the percentage of correctly predicted instances out of the total instances, providing a straightforward indication of model performance. Precision evaluates the accuracy of positive predictions, while recall assesses the model's ability to identify all relevant instances. F1-score, a balance between precision and recall, offers a more comprehensive view of model efficacy.

Analyzing these metrics helps identify areas where the model excels or requires improvement. For instance, if your model achieves high accuracy but low recall, it may indicate a tendency to overlook certain classes, suggesting the need for algorithm adjustments or data reevaluation.

To further enhance practical understanding, let's consider another example: customer sentiment analysis. Classification models can be used to categorize social media posts or product reviews based on sentiment, such as positive, negative, or neutral. By applying techniques similar to those in spam detection, businesses can automate the process of gauging customer opinions, driving strategic decisions and improving customer engagement.

It's important to note that building an effective classification model is an iterative process. As you gain experience, experimenting with different algorithms, tuning hyperparameters, and exploring advanced techniques like ensemble methods can significantly improve model performance. Documenting each step and result enables continuous learning and refinement of classification skills.

Moreover, practical application guidelines can complement theoretical understanding. When embarking on real-world projects, start small and iterate incrementally. Always keep the end goal in sight: to deliver solutions that truly address specific problems or enhance existing processes. Emphasizing usability ensures that your classification models have tangible impacts, aligning technological exploration with practical utility.

Creating a Chatbot Using Basic AI Tools

In today's digital landscape, chatbots are increasingly prevalent across various sectors, providing efficient customer service and enhancing user engagement. Understanding the fundamentals of chatbot creation is crucial for anyone looking to harness the power of AI in practical applications. This subpoint focuses on equipping readers with essential knowledge about designing interaction-rich chatbots and integrating AI seamlessly into their operations.

To begin with, it's important to distinguish between different types of chatbots and understand their operations. Chatbots can generally be categorized into three main types: rule-based, AI-driven, and hybrid models. Rule-based chatbots follow a pre-defined set of rules and are suitable for straightforward interactions where the conversation path is predictable. In contrast, AI-driven chatbots leverage machine learning algorithms to interpret and respond to complex user inputs, making them more adaptable and capable of understanding context. Hybrid chatbots combine aspects of both rule-based and AI-driven models, offering flexibility and scalability in application. Each type has its unique use cases— rule-based bots are often used for FAQ responses, whereas AI-driven bots excel in nuanced customer support roles.

Developing a successful chatbot involves more than selecting the right type; it requires meticulous attention to interaction design. Crafting an effective dialogue flow is paramount. Begin by mapping out potential conversation scenarios that users might engage in. User-centric design principles should guide this process, ensuring the bot's responses are intuitive and natural. Consider response variations to maintain engagement and prevent interactions from feeling monotonous or scripted. A chatbot that can handle diverse queries with coherence is more likely to enhance user satisfaction.

Integrating AI into your chatbot doesn't necessitate extensive coding expertise. Various platforms offer tools that simplify this process, allowing beginners and professionals alike to implement AI features with minimal effort. For instance, platforms like Dialogflow, Microsoft Bot Framework, and IBM Watson provide user-friendly interfaces where you can create and deploy chatbots without needing deep technical know-how. These platforms often come with tutorials and templates to help you get started quickly. By leveraging these resources, you can focus on refining your chatbot's functionality instead of getting bogged down in complex programming tasks.

Once your chatbot is operational, continuous testing and improvement are crucial to its success. Regularly gather user feedback to gain insights into how the bot is performing and where it may fall short. Analytics can play a significant role here; by tracking metrics like response time, user engagement levels, and conversation drop-off points, you can identify areas needing enhancement. Implement A/B testing to experiment with different response strategies and dialogue flows to determine what works best for your audience. Remember, a well-optimized chatbot not only answers queries efficiently but also evolves based on user interactions to provide an ever-improving experience.

Analyzing Data Sets: Predictions and Patterns

Delving into the world of data analysis begins with understanding the transformation of raw data into actionable insights. Raw data, in its unprocessed form, holds immense potential but requires careful handling to become truly useful. The process starts with data collection, followed by cleaning and preprocessing to remove noise and inaccuracies that may skew results. This preparative work ensures that the data is accurate, complete, and ready for further analysis.

Once the data is primed, Exploratory Data Analysis (EDA) comes into play as a powerful technique to uncover patterns and relationships within the dataset. EDA employs both statistical tools and data visualization techniques to summarize the main characteristics of the data. Through plots such as histograms, scatter plots, and box plots, you can visually detect trends, outliers, and underlying structures. For beginners, tools like Python's Pandas and Matplotlib offer an accessible entry point into EDA, enabling users to manipulate datasets and generate insightful visualizations without extensive coding experience.

In addition to visual exploration, EDA also involves using statistical measures to delve deeper into the data. Descriptive statistics such as mean, median, variance, and standard deviation provide numerical summaries of the data's central tendency and dispersion. By exploring how the data is distributed, practitioners can develop hypotheses about what the data is indicating, setting the stage for more sophisticated analyses.

Transitioning from exploration to prediction, predictive modeling forms the backbone of many data-driven decision-making processes. Predictive modeling uses historical data to forecast future outcomes or behaviors, and it is crucial across various domains, including finance, healthcare, and marketing. One fundamental concept here is feature selection, which involves identifying the most relevant data attributes that contribute to the predictive power of the model. Careful selection of features not only enhances model performance but also helps in reducing complexity and computational costs.

An essential consideration during predictive modeling is avoiding the pitfall of overfitting. Overfitting occurs when a model learns the detail and noise in the training data to an extent that it negatively impacts the model's performance on new data. It effectively memorizes the training set rather than learning a pattern that generalizes to unseen data. To combat overfitting, techniques such as cross-validation, regularization, and pruning are employed, helping ensure that models maintain a balance between accuracy and adaptability.

Bridging theory with practice, it's important to see how data analysis translates into practical outcomes through case studies across industries. In the retail industry, for instance, companies use predictive analytics to anticipate customer buying behaviors, optimize inventory management, and personalize marketing strategies. By analyzing patterns in their data, these businesses make informed decisions that directly impact profitability and customer satisfaction. Similarly, in healthcare, predictive modeling aids in patient diagnosis and treatment planning by analyzing medical histories and identifying risk factors for diseases.

Another compelling case is within financial services, where banks employ data analysis to assess credit risk and detect fraudulent activities. By integrating EDA and predictive modeling, financial institutions can enhance their ability to predict defaults and mitigate risks, ensuring improved security and reliability for their customers. These real-world examples not only illustrate the versatility of data analysis but also emphasize the tangible benefits it offers across varied contexts.

For educators and students eager to incorporate AI concepts into curricula or projects, introducing exercises that apply these techniques in controlled environments can significantly enhance understanding. Practical assignments that involve working with open-source datasets, such as those available from public repositories, can be particularly effective. They provide hands-on experience with data manipulation, visualization, and modeling, bridging the gap between theoretical knowledge and practical application.

Moreover, professionals seeking to elevate their skills will find that engaging with these exercises not only improves proficiency in technical tools but also builds a mindset attuned to making data-driven decisions. As AI and data analysis continue to permeate all sectors, having foundational skills in analyzing and interpreting data becomes increasingly indispensable.

Experimenting with Image Recognition

Image recognition is one of the most fascinating areas of artificial intelligence, and it's something you've likely experienced without realizing it. At its core, image recognition involves teaching computers to understand visual data—pictures and videos—much like humans do. This technology powers many applications we use daily, including self-driving cars, which rely on their ability to interpret the surrounding environment by recognizing objects, pedestrians, and road signs. Image recognition also plays a role in facial recognition systems, medical imaging, and even photo tagging on social media platforms.

To start exploring image recognition, you'll need the right tools. Fortunately, there are several accessible options for beginners that make it easy to experiment without needing extensive programming knowledge or deep technical expertise. TensorFlow, an open-source machine learning framework developed by Google, offers a user-friendly entry point. It allows you to access pre-trained models, which are AI models that have already been trained on vast amounts of data, saving you time and effort. These models can be used as starting points for your own image recognition projects, allowing you to test ideas quickly and see how altering certain parameters can lead to improved results.

A simple but effective way to get hands-on with image recognition is by building your own application. Imagine creating a tool that can analyze images and identify objects within them—a basic image classification application. To achieve this, follow a structured exercise: first, gather a set of labeled images relevant to the object categories you wish to recognize, such as animals, vehicles, or fruits. Utilize a platform like TensorFlow to leverage a pre-trained model, such as MobileNet, which balances performance and efficiency well. With some customization, including fine-tuning the model's parameters and retraining it with your dataset, you will have a practical image recognition application ready to go.

Real-life applications of image recognition are vast and ever-expanding across various industries. In healthcare, for example, image recognition aids radiologists in diagnosing diseases by detecting abnormalities in medical scans with impressive accuracy and speed. In retail, automated checkout systems utilize this technology to recognize items and simplify the purchasing process. However, as image recognition becomes more integrated into society, ethical considerations must be addressed. Issues such as privacy concerns, biases present in datasets, and the potential misuse of surveillance technology require thoughtful consideration and careful regulation to ensure fair and responsible use.

Practical Applications Across Industries

Artificial intelligence (AI) is transforming industries by allowing them to harness the power of data and make informed decisions. One notable application is classification, which enhances decision-making in sectors like healthcare, finance, and marketing. By categorizing data efficiently, classification models help businesses predict customer preferences, identify fraudulent activities, and even aid doctors in diagnosing diseases. For instance, in finance, AI-driven classification can detect patterns of fraudulent transactions by analyzing massive datasets, a task previously overwhelming for human analysts. Moving into healthcare, AI algorithms classify medical images and biological samples, improving diagnosis speed and accuracy.

Moreover, chatbots have revolutionized how companies engage with customers and improve operational efficiencies. By automating routine inquiries, chatbots provide instant assistance, freeing human agents to handle complex issues. This technology not only reduces response times but also operates 24/7, offering continuous support. Retailers use chatbots to guide users through product selections, while financial institutions deploy them to manage account queries. Their ability to process natural language ensures personalized interactions, enhancing customer satisfaction.

Data-driven insights form the foundation of strategic decisions across various fields. Businesses leverage AI to turn raw data into actionable insights, refining their approaches and strategies. In retail, customer shopping patterns and preferences are analyzed to optimize inventory management and tailor marketing efforts. The automotive industry uses AI to monitor vehicle health and driving habits, paving the way for predictive maintenance and enhanced safety measures. By equipping professionals with these analytical tools, AI empowers them to base decisions on concrete evidence rather than intuition alone.

Image recognition technology is another domain constantly evolving due to AI's influence. Innovations in this field are reshaping industries from security to entertainment. Surveillance systems now include facial recognition capabilities, aiding law enforcement in identifying individuals and maintaining public safety. Additionally, social media platforms employ image recognition to streamline content moderation, ensuring compliance with community standards. As the technology matures, it's expected to drive other innovations, such as augmented reality experiences and advanced visual search engines.

The future of AI holds great potential as trends continue to push boundaries. Image recognition, for example, could revolutionize healthcare by enabling precise and non-invasive diagnostics through medical imaging. Fashion retailers might utilize this technology for virtual try-ons, offering personalized experiences to customers. Moreover, advancements in this field could lead to improvements in autonomous vehicles, where real-time image processing ensures safe navigation and obstacle detection. These developments not only promise innovative applications but also pose ethical questions about privacy and data security, prompting ongoing discussions in the tech community.

CHAPTER 8

Integrating AI in Professional

Workspaces

Integrating AI into professional workspaces is a transformative process that can significantly enhance operational efficiency and productivity. As businesses continue to evolve in a rapidly changing digital landscape, the incorporation of artificial intelligence offers numerous opportunities to streamline processes and optimize resources. By carefully selecting tasks for AI automation, organizations can harness the power of technology to reduce repetitive workloads and allow employees to focus on more strategic endeavors. This shift not only drives innovation but also helps in maintaining a competitive edge in various industries. Understanding which tasks are apt for AI intervention is crucial, as it lays the foundation for successful integration and maximizes the benefits of this advanced technology. Identifying suitable tasks involves a methodical approach, ensuring that AI solutions align with organizational goals and enhance overall performance.

This chapter delves into the essential techniques for effectively incorporating AI into different professional settings. Readers will gain practical insights into evaluating tasks for AI automation using structured approaches such as task analysis frameworks. The content emphasizes the importance of prioritizing tasks that offer significant benefits when automated, thus improving time management and reducing error rates. Additionally, the chapter explains how engaging employees in the AI adoption process fosters acceptance and smoothens transitions within the workplace. Furthermore, the chapter explores the use of tools like AI workload analysis software and process mapping, which guide organizations in assessing workflow efficiency. Through these discussions, readers will be equipped with a comprehensive understanding of how AI can be integrated into their work environment, leading to improved accuracy, efficiency, and strategic utilization of human resources.

Identifying Tasks Suitable for AI Automation

Incorporating artificial intelligence (AI) into professional workspaces offers significant potential for improving efficiency and productivity. To effectively leverage AI, it is crucial to identify tasks within your organization that are suitable candidates for automation. A structured approach to evaluating tasks can help achieve this goal, guiding organizations in making informed decisions.

A useful starting point is learning a task analysis framework, which provides a methodical way to evaluate tasks based on their characteristics and feasibility for AI automation. This approach emphasizes focusing on repetitive and rule-based tasks. These are tasks that follow a set sequence of operations or rely heavily on logic and rules, such as data entry, invoice processing, and standard reporting. By identifying these repetitive processes, organizations can pinpoint areas where AI can take over, freeing up human resources for more strategic activities.

When using a task analysis framework, it's important to consider the unique aspects of your organization's workflows. Each task should be carefully examined to determine its suitability for automation. Factors such as complexity, variability, and data availability play key roles. For instance, a task with minimal variation and ample clean data is more likely to be a successful candidate for AI automation. By systematically applying this framework, organizations can make objective decisions about which tasks are ripe for automation.

Beyond identification, organizations need to prioritize tasks that will offer the most significant benefits when automated. A critical part of this process is determining which tasks consume the most time or are prone to frequent errors. Strategies that assess these factors help in singling out tasks whose automation could lead to high returns in terms of time savings and reduction in costly errors. For example, customer support inquiries that require standardized responses can be efficiently managed through AI, significantly reducing response times while minimizing human error.

Assessing the potential impact of automation includes weighing the costs and benefits. Organizations should consider not only the immediate gains but also the long-term advantages of improved accuracy and efficiency. Prioritizing tasks with the highest return on investment ensures that the initial efforts and resources poured into AI integration bring measurable benefits to the organization.

Engaging employees in the automation process is equally important. Their involvement fosters acceptance and embraces the changes introduced by AI technologies. Encouraging collaborative brainstorming sessions allows employees to share insights about daily operations, helping identify pain points and suggesting potential improvements. This inclusive approach boosts morale and makes employees feel valued, transforming them from passive observers to active participants in the transformation journey.

Moreover, involving team members in the transition builds trust and understanding. Employees who understand how AI will augment their roles are more likely to accept and support its implementation. Through transparent communication and training, organizations can manage change more effectively, ensuring a smooth transition to automated processes.

To evaluate task suitability for automation, organizations can utilize various tools and methodologies. AI workload analysis software helps assess current workflows to identify potential automation candidates. By analyzing patterns and workloads, these tools provide valuable insights into which tasks can be optimized through AI. Additionally, process mapping proves invaluable in visualizing and assessing workflow efficiency. It helps teams identify bottlenecks and areas of improvement, offering a clear path toward streamlining operations.

Using these tools, organizations can conduct comprehensive evaluations of their processes, building a solid foundation for successful AI integration. Moreover, these assessments often reveal unexpected opportunities for innovation and optimization beyond obvious candidates for automation.

Customizing AI Solutions for Business Needs

In today's rapidly changing business environment, integrating artificial intelligence (AI) can dramatically reshape how organizations operate, making them more agile and efficient. However, to truly harness the power of AI, companies must first adapt these technologies to their unique requirements and address specific organizational challenges.

The first step in tailoring AI solutions is understanding the specific needs of the organization. This involves gathering and analyzing relevant information about what the business requires from AI. Conducting stakeholder interviews offers invaluable insights into different perspectives within the company. By engaging with individuals from various departments and roles, you can better identify the pain points and areas that could benefit most from AI interventions. Additionally, compiling thorough documentation of business requirements helps create a comprehensive blueprint for AI integration. This ensures that every aspect of the company's operations is considered, leading to more targeted and effective AI solutions.

Once the organization's needs are clearly defined, it's important to approach the development of AI prototypes iteratively. An iterative process allows for fine-tuning and adjustments based on ongoing feedback and testing. The idea is to develop small-scale AI models tailored to specific tasks before scaling them up for full implementation. This method reduces risk by allowing teams to experiment and improve AI functionalities incrementally. For example, a company might start with a prototype AI aimed at customer service improvement, gradually enhancing its features based on employee and customer input until it achieves the desired level of performance. Through this approach, potential issues can be identified and resolved early, saving both time and resources in the long run.

Adapting existing AI tools to fit seamlessly into a business's workflow is another critical step. Often, off-the-shelf AI solutions may not align perfectly with an organization's operational processes. Modifying these tools to suit specific workflows requires a delicate balance between customization and maintaining vendor support. Altering an AI system too extensively might lead to compatibility issues or void support agreements. Therefore, when customizing AI applications, it's crucial to understand which modifications are feasible while still retaining the benefits of vendor updates and support. Tips for achieving this include collaborating closely with technology providers to understand the scope of allowable customizations and ensuring that internal IT teams have the necessary skills to implement changes without disrupting core functionalities.

Continuous feedback loops play an essential role in refining AI solutions post-implementation. After deploying an AI system, it's vital to monitor its performance continuously and remain receptive to user feedback. This feedback should inform ongoing adjustments and improvements, enhancing the AI's effectiveness over time. For instance, if users find a feature cumbersome or fail to engage with it as intended, developers can tweak it to better align with user expectations. Encouraging employees to provide regular feedback also fosters a collaborative culture that values user input, leading to higher satisfaction levels and improved AI utility within the organization.

Moreover, establishing metrics for evaluating AI performance allows businesses to track progress and make informed decisions about further adaptations. Regular assessments help identify areas where the AI falls short and determine necessary enhancements. These evaluations should be integrated into the normal operations cycle so that improvements can be addressed promptly. For example, a retail company using AI for inventory management might discover through performance metrics that the system's prediction accuracy decreases during seasonal peaks. Armed with this knowledge, the company can adjust the AI algorithm to better handle such fluctuations, thereby improving inventory efficiency.

Ensuring Seamless Integration with Existing Processes

Integrating new AI systems into pre-established organizational frameworks requires careful planning and strategic approaches to ensure seamless adoption without disrupting ongoing operations. The first step in achieving this involves developing integration planning strategies. These strategies should outline clear timelines, resource allocation, key milestones, and involve getting stakeholder buy-in. Establishing a timeline is crucial as it provides a structured approach to the implementation process, enabling organizations to set realistic goals and deadlines. It also helps allocate resources efficiently, ensuring that both human capital and technological tools are available when needed. Identifying key milestones assists in tracking progress and maintaining momentum throughout the integration efforts. Stakeholder involvement is critical because gaining their support can facilitate smoother transitions and foster acceptance of new technologies within the organization.

Understanding how AI solutions work harmoniously with existing software is another important aspect of successful integration. This can be achieved through the use of Application Programming Interfaces (APIs) and middleware solutions designed to facilitate interoperability between diverse systems. APIs serve as a bridge, allowing different software applications to communicate and share data seamlessly. Middleware solutions further enhance this communication by acting as intermediaries that manage interactions between disparate systems. For instance, if a company uses a legacy accounting system alongside new AI-driven analytics software, middleware can enable these systems to work together, ensuring that data is accurately shared, processed, and utilized for decision-making. By employing these technological solutions, organizations can create an integrated environment where new AI systems complement rather than disrupt existing workflows.

In addition to technical considerations, managing personnel transitions effectively is paramount when integrating AI into the workplace. Change management techniques play a vital role in this aspect. Effective communication stands at the forefront of successful change management. It involves informing employees about the objectives and benefits of AI integration and addressing any concerns they may have. Regular updates and open channels of communication can help build trust and reduce resistance to change. Furthermore, implementing training programs is essential to equip employees with the necessary skills to work alongside AI technologies. Providing hands-on learning opportunities, workshops, and resources can ease the transition and boost confidence among staff members. Resistance management is another critical component, as some employees may be apprehensive about AI's impact on job roles. By fostering a culture of transparency and inclusivity, organizations can encourage collaboration between employees and AI systems, ultimately leading to higher productivity and innovation.

Implementing AI pilot programs in stages is a practical approach to minimizing disruptions and refining processes based on feedback from pilot success. Pilot programs allow organizations to test AI systems in controlled environments before full-scale deployment. By launching these programs incrementally, businesses can identify potential challenges and gather insights into how AI performs within specific contexts. Feedback from pilot participants can provide valuable information for fine-tuning AI solutions and optimizing them to meet organizational needs. For example, a retail company testing AI for inventory management might conduct a pilot program in one store before expanding to others. This staged approach not only reduces risks but also enables organizations to learn from initial experiences and make informed decisions about scaling AI implementations.

Employee engagement is a crucial element that deserves special emphasis. Engaging employees in the AI integration process enhances their sense of involvement and ownership over changes that affect their daily work. It is vital to create an environment where employees feel comfortable sharing their thoughts and contributing ideas. Encouraging collaborative brainstorming sessions can generate fresh perspectives and innovative solutions, fostering a sense of camaraderie among teams. Involving employees in discussions about AI's potential benefits, such as automating repetitive tasks or improving data analysis, can shift perceptions from apprehension to enthusiasm. Demonstrating how AI aligns with organizational goals and improves overall efficiency helps garner support and commitment from staff members.

Measuring Success and ROI of AI Implementations

Tracking the effectiveness and return on investment (ROI) of AI initiatives is crucial for organizations looking to enhance efficiency and maintain a competitive edge. By systematically evaluating AI performance through key performance indicators (KPIs), businesses can align AI efforts with their strategic goals, ensuring modifications are made when necessary. Selecting the right KPIs is essential as they serve as benchmarks to measure progress and success. Businesses should focus on indicators that reflect the specific outcomes they hope to achieve with AI, such as operational efficiency, cost savings, or enhanced customer satisfaction. For instance, an organization looking to improve customer service using AI chatbots might track metrics like response time or resolution rates.

Calculating the financial impact of AI implementations involves both tangible and intangible factors, where cost-benefit analysis becomes a powerful tool. Tangible ROI includes direct financial returns such as increased revenue or reduced costs from automated processes. Intangible benefits might involve improved brand reputation or customer experience. Frameworks for cost-benefit analysis help in quantifying these elements, providing a clearer picture of AI's value proposition. For example, a retail company implementing AI-driven inventory management would assess both the reduction in excess stock (tangible) and the improved customer satisfaction from better product availability (intangible).

Continuous feedback loops play a pivotal role in enhancing AI effectiveness over time. By consistently collecting and analyzing data on AI performance, organizations can identify areas for improvement and adapt their strategies accordingly. This process fosters a culture of continuous learning and innovation, enabling businesses to refine their AI solutions iteratively. In practice, this could mean regularly updating an AI model based on user feedback or new market trends, thus ensuring it remains relevant and effective. A tech company might use customer feedback to upgrade its voice recognition software, addressing issues of accuracy and speed based on user experiences.

Effective reporting and stakeholder communication are integral to transparently presenting AI performance and engaging stakeholders in discussions aimed at improvement. By developing best practices for reporting, organizations not only account for their AI initiatives but also build trust with stakeholders. Regular reports should highlight KPI achievements, financial impacts, and insights gained from feedback loops, offering a comprehensive view of AI performance. Consider a healthcare provider that integrates AI into patient care; detailed reporting on treatment outcomes, patient feedback, and operational efficiencies communicates clear value to stakeholders, fostering collaboration and support for further AI-driven innovations.

In achieving these goals, guidelines become particularly helpful when identifying effective KPIs and constructing cost-benefit analyses. For instance, using tools designed for task identification assists in pinpointing appropriate KPIs that accurately reflect AI's contribution to business objectives. Similarly, applying structured frameworks ensures that all potential financial impacts are considered comprehensively. By adhering to established guidelines, organizations can navigate the complexities of integrating AI with greater precision and confidence.

The overall strategy of tracking AI investments must be dynamic, adapting to changes in technology and market demands. Organizations need to remain flexible, updating KPIs, revisiting cost calculations, and refining feedback mechanisms as needed. The ultimate aim is to ensure that AI initiatives do not stagnate but instead continuously contribute to organizational growth and competitiveness.

Tools and Approaches for Evaluating Task Suitability

In today's professional landscape, integrating AI into workspaces is becoming increasingly essential. One of the initial steps in this process is identifying tasks that can be automated through AI. Software and methodologies play a crucial role here by helping identify areas where AI integration would be most beneficial.

To start with, AI tools for workload analysis are pivotal in understanding which duties within an organization could be automated. These tools analyze various data points related to daily operations, providing insights into repetitive tasks that consume significant time and resources. For instance, tools like Asana and Monday.com offer advanced analytics features that track task durations, frequency, and complexity. By interpreting this data, companies can ascertain which functions are ripe for automation, thereby optimizing workflow efficiency and allowing human employees to focus on more strategic tasks.

Next, another effective method is process mapping, which serves as a critical tool in identifying potential candidates for automation. Process mapping involves creating detailed flowcharts or diagrams that outline every step involved in a workflow. This visual representation makes it easier to spot redundant or time-consuming steps that could benefit from automation. Tools such as Lucidchart and Microsoft Visio offer robust features for creating and analyzing process maps. When organizations map out their internal processes, they can systematically examine each segment's necessity, often discovering that many tasks could be streamlined or automated altogether.

Moreover, several platforms are specifically designed to monitor tasks for automation potential, assisting in efficient decision-making processes. Platforms like UiPath and Automation Anywhere not only automate existing processes but also provide dashboards to track performance metrics and operational impacts pre- and post-automation. By leveraging these platforms, businesses gain valuable statistics about how certain tasks perform over time and whether these tasks meet the criteria for effective AI-driven automation.

In exploring successful integrations, case studies across different sectors highlight the advantages of identifying suitable automation tasks. In the finance industry, companies such as JPMorgan Chase have employed AI tools for processing loan applications, significantly reducing the manual workload and speeding up approval times. Similarly, logistics firms like DHL have utilized AI to automate warehouse sorting processes, improving accuracy and efficiency while cutting costs. These examples illustrate the tangible benefits of carefully selecting which tasks to automate: increased productivity, reduced operational expenses, and enhanced employee satisfaction.

These cases underscore the importance of following a structured approach when incorporating AI. To ensure you're focusing on the right areas, it's vital to first understand your organization's specific needs and capacity for change. While AI presents a plethora of opportunities, jumping into automation without thorough preparation can lead to challenges such as improper scaling or misaligned expectations. Hence, it's advisable to begin with pilot projects that target manageable parts of a business, gather feedback, and iterate based on results. This methodology helps refine strategies, making subsequent larger-scale implementations smoother and more effective. When examining AI tools for workload analysis, remember they not only identify current inefficiencies but also predict future trends in task management. As AI continually learns from data inputs, its ability to foresee patterns or bottlenecks enhances over time. This predictive capability allows organizations to stay ahead of potential disruptions, ensuring that they can adapt and evolve proactively rather than reactively. In this sense, investing in AI tools is not just about addressing immediate needs but also about building resilience and agility for future growth.

Process mapping further complements these efforts by fostering a culture of transparency and continuous improvement within teams. By involving team members in the mapping exercises, organizations encourage a collaborative environment where employees feel empowered to contribute ideas and insights. Engaging staff in this manner does more than streamline workflows; it cultivates a sense of ownership and shared purpose, which is instrumental in driving innovation and embracing technological advancements.

Adding to this, regularly reviewing platforms that support task monitoring ensures that AI solutions remain relevant and effective. The dynamic nature of technology means that capabilities improve rapidly, and staying updated with the latest advancements allows businesses to maximize their investments in AI. Regular evaluations and updates are necessary to harness new features or integrate additional functionalities that align with evolving business goals.

CHAPTER 9

Ethics and Future of AI

E thics and the future of artificial intelligence (AI) are central to the ongoing discourse about technology's role in society. The integration of AI into various sectors presents both opportunities and challenges, particularly when it comes to ensuring ethical use. As AI continues to develop, questions about fairness, bias, and responsibility are becoming more prevalent. These considerations are crucial as they impact how AI systems interact with diverse communities and influence decision-making processes. The pursuit of responsible AI development is not only a technical challenge but also an ethical imperative that requires a collective effort from developers, policymakers, and educators alike.

In this chapter, we delve into the various ethical considerations associated with AI, focusing particularly on issues of bias and fairness. Readers will explore how biases emerge in AI systems, often reflecting historical data patterns that can lead to unintended discrimination. We'll examine the importance of creating diverse datasets and conducting regular audits to mitigate these biases. This chapter also emphasizes interdisciplinary collaboration, highlighting the roles of ethicists and social scientists in framing technical solutions within ethical contexts. Through real-world examples and guidelines for developing robust frameworks, we aim to provide a comprehensive understanding of how ethical principles can guide AI's future trajectory. The content presented is designed to equip readers— be they beginners, professionals, or educators—with the knowledge needed to engage with AI responsibly and harness its potential for societal benefit.

Addressing Bias in AI Models

In recent years, artificial intelligence (AI) has become an integral part of many sectors, from healthcare and finance to transportation and entertainment. However, with its growing influence comes the critical challenge of ensuring these systems operate fairly and without bias. At the heart of this issue is the tendency for AI algorithms to inherit biases present in their underlying data or flawed algorithmic design. Such biases, if unchecked, can lead to discrimination and reinforce unfair stereotypes, impacting individuals and communities on a significant scale.

Bias in AI is not always an intentional result but often stems from historical patterns encoded in datasets. For instance, if an AI system is trained on a dataset that lacks diversity or over-represents certain demographic groups, it may make incorrect assumptions about underrepresented groups. This misrepresentation can manifest in various ways, such as skewed hiring decisions, biased credit evaluations, or even profiling in law enforcement, all of which have profound societal implications.

To combat these inherent biases, diverse datasets are essential for training AI models. It's analogous to creating a balanced diet—just as one needs a variety of nutrients for optimal health, AI requires varied and representative data to function fairly. Implementing regular audits of AI systems is another crucial step in identifying and mitigating biases. These audits involve scrutinizing both the data fed into the system and the outcomes generated to ensure they align with ethical standards.

While the idea of conducting audits may seem daunting, it's a necessary measure for maintaining the credibility of AI technologies. Moreover, audits create a space for continuous learning and improvement, where biases are not only identified but also addressed systematically. By integrating checks at every stage of AI development—from data collection to deployment—developers can substantially reduce instances of bias.

Real-world case studies provide insight into the ramifications of biased AI and underscore the urgency of addressing these issues. Take, for example, the case of an AI-based recruitment tool used by a tech giant, which was found to favor male applicants due to historical patterns in their previous hiring data. This situation highlighted how AI systems could perpetuate existing gender disparities in the workforce if not carefully managed. By examining such scenarios, we glean valuable lessons on the necessity of vigilance and rectification in AI applications.

These examples emphasize the need for interdisciplinary collaboration. Data scientists alone cannot tackle bias issues; ethicists and social scientists play a pivotal role. They bring unique perspectives and expertise that help frame technical solutions within ethical contexts. This collaborative synergy can yield AI models that are not only technically robust but morally sound. Such partnerships foster environments where fairness is prioritized alongside performance.

Guidelines for building robust frameworks to evaluate bias are vital for promoting fairness in AI. These frameworks serve as blueprints, assisting developers in recognizing potential biases and implementing corrective measures. They encourage the inclusion of impact assessments at each phase of AI construction, which involves evaluating the broader societal effects of AI decisions. This proactive approach ensures that AI systems evolve in a manner consistent with ethical values and public trust.

The challenges presented by bias in AI algorithms serve as a crucial reminder of the responsibilities borne by developers and organizations. As AI continues to shape various aspects of daily life, the pursuit of fairness must remain at the forefront of technological advancements. Organizations are encouraged to adopt guidelines that stress the importance of ethical considerations in AI model design, engaging with a broad spectrum of stakeholders throughout the process.

Moreover, diversity in the teams developing AI systems is fundamental to minimizing biases. A varied team brings different viewpoints and experiences, reducing the likelihood of oversight in addressing bias. Inclusivity in AI development thus parallels the necessity of inclusive data—both are essential for creating equitable and reliable AI systems.

Fostering education and training in ethical AI practices is another key aspect of addressing bias. This involves equipping current and future professionals with the skills and knowledge to recognize and mitigate bias effectively. Educational programs should incorporate discussions on the ethical use of technology, highlighting the importance of critical evaluation and responsible innovation.

It becomes imperative for governments, organizations, and educational institutions to collectively uphold accountability in AI through transparent practices and policies. This involves setting standards and regulations that promote fair AI usage while encouraging innovative exploration. Balancing regulation with creativity allows society to harness the benefits of AI responsibly, leading to more equitable outcomes across various domains.

Ultimately, the successful integration of fairness into AI systems will determine the level of trust and acceptance they receive from the public. By consciously addressing biases and embedding fairness at the core of AI development, we ensure that these technologies contribute positively to society, enhancing rather than hindering our collective progress.

Privacy Concerns in AI Implementation

In recent years, artificial intelligence has transformed many aspects of our lives, from personal assistants that voice our inquiries to targeted ads that seem to read our minds. But as AI technologies grow more advanced, they increasingly rely on the massive collection and processing of personal data. This dependence raises critical privacy concerns that urgently need ethical consideration. Understanding these issues is vital for anyone involved in AI development or use.

AI's reliance on personal data is largely because machine learning models require vast amounts of data to learn and improve. Personal data provides the nuanced insights needed to tailor algorithms so they can make accurate predictions and better decisions. However, this necessity brings about significant privacy challenges. For instance, the accumulation and analysis of sensitive information such as health records, financial transactions, and browsing habits could result in misuse if not appropriately managed. Unauthorized access or data breaches can lead to severe consequences, including identity theft and unwanted surveillance.

Addressing these privacy concerns involves a firm grasp of existing regulations like the General Data Protection Regulation (GDPR). GDPR, introduced by the European Union, sets a high standard for data protection worldwide, requiring organizations to safeguard the personal information they collect and process. It gives individuals control over their data with rights such as access, rectification, and erasure. Compliance with GDPR is not just a matter of adhering to legal obligations; it embodies the principles of transparency, accountability, and trust between technology creators and users. For example, companies must implement privacy by design, embedding robust data protection measures throughout their systems.

To further protect individual privacy within AI systems, there are several techniques worth exploring, such as anonymization and encryption. Anonymization involves altering personal data so it cannot be traced back to an individual, ensuring that even if data is breached, it remains useless to unauthorized entities. Encryption, on the other hand, converts data into a coded format, making it inaccessible without the correct decryption key. These techniques help mitigate risks associated with data privacy while allowing AI systems to function effectively. For example, medical researchers can use anonymized patient data to develop life-saving AI-based treatments without compromising patient confidentiality.

Public sentiment surrounding privacy issues will undoubtedly influence the trajectory of future AI technologies. As people become more aware of how their data is utilized, there is growing demand for greater transparency and control over personal information. Companies that fail to address these concerns might face backlash or loss of consumer trust. Alternatively, organizations that prioritize privacy and foster an open dialogue about their data practices are likely to gain a competitive edge. For instance, tech giants like Apple have made privacy a core part of their brand identity, offering features that allow users to manage app permissions and tracking options easily.

As AI technologies continue to evolve, striking the right balance between innovation and privacy protection becomes crucial. Developers and policymakers play a pivotal role in ensuring that AI advances responsibly and benefits society as a whole. On one hand, developers should build systems with privacy at their core, incorporating cutting-edge security measures and maintaining transparency in their operations. On the other, regulators must adapt existing laws to keep pace with technological advancements, ensuring they remain effective in safeguarding personal data.

Moving forward, we need a collaborative effort involving researchers, technologists, legislators, and citizens. Educating consumers about their rights and how their data is used contributes to a well-informed public capable of advocating for stronger privacy protections. Meanwhile, fostering partnerships between industries and governments can drive the creation of robust frameworks that protect individuals while supporting technological growth.

Regulatory Frameworks and Compliance

In the dynamic field of artificial intelligence (AI), regulatory frameworks play a crucial role in safeguarding against potential misuse. As AI continues to evolve, it is becoming more integrated into diverse aspects of society, underscoring the need for clear guidelines and legislation to protect societal interests. Regulations ensure that AI technologies are developed and implemented in ways that do not compromise ethical standards or public safety.

A prominent example of regulatory efforts is the European Union's AI Act, which aims to establish a comprehensive set of rules governing the use of AI across member states. The EU AI Act categorizes AI systems based on risk levels, ranging from minimal risk to unacceptable risk, with specific requirements for each category. This structured approach ensures that high-risk AI applications, such as those used in critical infrastructure or law enforcement, undergo stringent scrutiny. By setting clear boundaries, the Act seeks to mitigate potential harms while fostering innovation within safe parameters.

Organizations operating within regions impacted by such legislative measures must adapt to comply with these regulations. Compliance is not just about avoiding legal repercussions; it is an opportunity to build trust with consumers and stakeholders. Companies must establish robust compliance strategies, incorporating regular audits and assessments to ensure adherence to new laws. This involves staying updated with changes in legislation and understanding their implications for AI implementation.

Moreover, developing internal policies that align with external regulations can help organizations navigate this complex landscape effectively.

Balancing regulation with innovation presents both challenges and opportunities. On one hand, excessive regulation could stifle creativity and hinder technological advancements. On the other hand, too little oversight leaves room for unethical practices that could damage public trust. Striking the right balance allows for continued growth in AI development while ensuring that ethical practices are maintained. This equilibrium invites innovation by creating a stable environment where companies can explore new ideas without compromising on integrity.

In practice, achieving this balance requires collaboration between regulators, industry leaders, and other stakeholders. Open dialogues can lead to regulatory frameworks that accommodate emerging technologies while maintaining essential safeguards. This collaborative approach encourages the sharing of best practices and helps identify gaps in existing regulations, promoting a more adaptive and future-ready regulatory environment. In turn, organizations can leverage the stability provided by sound regulation to invest in AI initiatives confidently.

For professionals in technology and AI, understanding these regulatory structures is paramount. Whether you're developing AI tools or integrating them into your business operations, knowledge of relevant legislation ensures compliance and boosts competitiveness. Staying informed about global trends and regional specifics in AI regulation enables more strategic decision-making and opens up avenues for responsible innovation.

Educators and students pursuing careers in STEM fields also benefit from grasping the significance of AI regulations. Incorporating these discussions into curricula equips students with insights into the intersection of technology, ethics, and policy. Future professionals are thus prepared to contribute meaningfully to AI advancements, considering both the technical and ethical dimensions of their work.

To foster ethical AI development, organizations might focus on creating transparent data-handling processes, implementing bias mitigation strategies, and ensuring accountability in AI systems. Regulatory bodies often encourage these practices through guidelines that stress transparency and fairness. While specific laws may vary between regions, the overarching goal remains consistent: to harness AI's potential responsibly for the collective good.

Moreover, there is a tangible value in organizations proactively engaging with regulatory processes. Participation in consultations or providing feedback on proposed regulations can shape favorable outcomes for industries and communities alike. By influencing policy development, organizations can advocate for realistic and sustainable approaches that reflect the practical realities of AI deployment.

Ultimately, the future of AI regulation lies in its ability to be flexible and responsive. As AI technologies continue to evolve rapidly, so too must the frameworks governing them. It is vital for stakeholders across sectors to maintain a proactive stance, anticipating changes and adapting practices accordingly. Through cooperation and vigilant attention to regulatory shifts, the tech industry can drive forward responsibly, ensuring that AI remains a force for positive transformation in society.

The Evolving Landscape of AI Research

Advancements in artificial intelligence are rapidly transforming the technological landscape, with significant developments in areas like reinforcement learning and explainable AI. Reinforcement learning, a subset of machine learning, focuses on how agents should take actions in an environment to maximize cumulative rewards. This method has shown great promise in developing autonomous systems capable of learning complex tasks, from robotics to gaming. By continuously interacting with their environments, these systems can make decisions that improve over time, which is crucial for creating more responsive and intelligent AI solutions.

Explainable AI, on the other hand, addresses one of the most critical concerns in modern AI systems: transparency. As AI models become more complex, understanding their decision-making process becomes increasingly difficult. Explainable AI seeks to make AI processes more understandable to humans by providing clear explanations of how conclusions are reached. This transparency is essential for gaining trust in AI systems, especially in sectors like healthcare and finance where decisions may significantly impact human lives. By opening up the AI's decision pathways, users can verify outcomes, leading to greater confidence in the technology.

Cross-disciplinary collaborations between academia and industry play a pivotal role in enhancing AI capabilities and ensuring they align with societal needs. Academia brings theoretical insights and novel research methodologies, while industry provides practical applications and scaling opportunities. This symbiotic relationship fosters innovation and accelerates the implementation of AI technologies in real-world scenarios. Universities and companies working together on projects encourage knowledge exchange and application of cutting-edge research. For instance, joint initiatives in smart city development leverage AI for efficient public transport management, energy utilization, and resource distribution, ultimately benefiting society as a whole. Incorporating ethical considerations into AI research projects is not just advisable but imperative to prevent harmful outcomes. The ethical framework for AI ensures that technology adheres to principles such as fairness, accountability, and transparency. This is particularly important in avoiding discrimination or bias within AI systems that could disproportionately affect certain groups. By embedding ethics at every stage of development, researchers and developers can mitigate risks and design AI that respects user privacy and autonomy. Consider the example of self-driving cars, where ethical dilemmas involving life-and-death decisions must be navigated carefully. A robust ethical foundation helps guide the development of algorithms that prioritize the safety of both passengers and pedestrians alike. Moreover, ethical oversight committees within organizations can review AI projects, suggesting modifications to align with broader societal values, thereby reducing potential negative impacts.

The rapid pace of AI development demands adaptive strategies from stakeholders, including policymakers, educators, and industry leaders. With AI technologies advancing swiftly, it is crucial to develop frameworks that can adapt to new challenges and opportunities. Policymakers must stay informed about current trends to propose regulations that safeguard against misuse while fostering innovation. Educators must continuously update curricula to prepare students adequately for emerging roles in the tech industry. Industry leaders need to adopt agile approaches that allow quick responses to changes in technology and market demands.

For example, in education, adapting teaching methods to include AI literacy ensures that future generations are well-equipped to navigate a world where AI plays a central role. Workshops, online courses, and interactive modules can make AI concepts accessible to learners of all backgrounds, increasing their employability and understanding of this transformative field.

In industry, implementing flexible policies that support ongoing employee training and development in AI-related skills helps maintain competitiveness. Companies embracing lifelong learning cultures can better respond to technological shifts and capitalize on new AI-driven business opportunities.

Future Directions and Implications

The landscape of artificial intelligence (AI) is rapidly evolving, with its potential to transform various aspects of society becoming increasingly evident. As AI technology advances, it becomes imperative for individuals engaged in this field to remain informed about ethical practices. Continuous education in ethical AI is a cornerstone for preparing future professionals in the field. The dynamics of AI are ever-changing, and this fluidity necessitates a robust understanding of ethical frameworks. Educational programs focusing on AI must adapt to include courses that emphasize moral reasoning, case studies of past AI failures, and discussions around bias and fairness. Such an educational focus ensures that upcoming professionals can navigate the intricate ethical terrains they'll face in their careers.

Innovations in AI also bring new methods of data usage, notably privacy-centric technologies like federated learning. Federated learning allows algorithms to learn from data distributed across multiple devices without transferring that data to a central server. This minimizes the risk of privacy breaches and offers a promising solution for industries handling sensitive information. By keeping data local, it maintains user privacy while still contributing to the development of robust AI models. Privacy-centric innovations are indispensable as they align technological growth with societal norms and values, reducing fears surrounding data misuse while enabling continuous AI advancement. Regulatory oversight has always played a pivotal role in shaping industry standards, and AI is no exception. New policies focusing on bias and privacy are poised to reshape AI development standards significantly. Regulatory bodies worldwide are recognizing the profound impact AI can have and are working towards establishing guidelines that enforce ethical usage. For instance, ensuring transparency in AI decision-making processes helps mitigate bias by allowing scrutiny and auditability. Additionally, privacy regulations compel organizations to develop systems that protect consumer information rigorously. These legal frameworks not only serve as protective barriers but also as catalysts for designing innovative AI solutions that are both effective and ethically sound.

An essential aspect of understanding AI's societal impacts is anticipating its integration into everyday life. From healthcare to transportation, AI's reach is expanding, affecting how people interact with technology daily. Proactive strategies for ethical research and development become crucial in this context. Stakeholders, including scientists, policymakers, and educators, need to collaborate to establish guidelines that avert potential harms while maximizing benefits. Creating inclusive environments for public discourse on AI ethics can also provide valuable insights, ensuring developments align with societal expectations.

Moreover, fostering an interdisciplinary approach involving ethicists, technologists, and legal experts can lead to more balanced views on how AI should evolve. This collaboration helps pinpoint ethical dilemmas early on and facilitates conversations that shape the trajectory of AI's growth. Engagement with diverse perspectives enriches the dialogue, promoting innovations that uphold core human values.

CHAPTER 10

Charting Your AI Learning Journey

In the field of artificial intelligence (AI), embarking on a learning journey requires strategic planning and thoughtful goal-setting. This dynamic area of study is vast, with concepts ranging from fundamental algorithms to advanced machine learning techniques. Setting a clear path for your AI education can pave the way for effective knowledge acquisition and practical skill development. By creating realistic objectives, learners can navigate this complex landscape more efficiently. It's about breaking down seemingly insurmountable challenges into manageable tasks that propel continuous growth and understanding.

This chapter delves into the essential strategies for building a productive AI learning framework. Readers will explore methods for setting realistic goals, such as utilizing the SMART framework—ensuring objectives are Specific, Measurable, Achievable, Relevant, and Time-bound. These principles guide learners towards tailoring educational plans fitted to their unique aspirations and current knowledge levels. The chapter goes further to discuss how breaking topics into smaller, digestible segments aids in mastery without overwhelming the learner. Additionally, it highlights the value of personalized learning paths, acknowledging individual backgrounds while aligning goals with future career opportunities in AI. Through these discussions, readers will be equipped with the tools needed to foster a structured learning journey that keeps pace with the ever-evolving AI domain.

Setting Realistic Learning Goals

In the realm of artificial intelligence (AI), learning effectively and efficiently is crucial, especially given the vastness and complexity of the field. One of the cornerstones for success in this journey is setting clear and achievable learning objectives. This approach serves not only to guide AI education but also to prevent learners from feeling overwhelmed by the extensive array of topics and technologies. By understanding and applying principles like the SMART framework—Specific, Measurable, Achievable, Relevant, and Time-bound goals—learners can structure their education path in a way that is both motivational and productive.

The SMART framework encourages learners to establish objectives that are well-defined and trackable, ensuring that each goal serves a distinct purpose within the broader educational plan. For instance, rather than aiming to simply "learn AI," a more specific goal might be to "gain proficiency in Python programming for machine learning applications within six months." This specificity not only makes the goal clearer but provides a measurable metric—proficiency in Python—while aligning it with relevant skills necessary for a career in AI. Additionally, breaking down this goal into smaller weekly or monthly tasks makes it more achievable and time-bound. Completing these incremental steps fosters motivation as learners experience tangible progress, which can be particularly rewarding in a field as intricate as AI.

Breaking down complex topics into smaller parts is another vital strategy that complements setting SMART goals. The sheer breadth of AI can be daunting, with subjects ranging from neural networks and natural language processing to robotics and computer vision. Tackling these topics all at once could lead to cognitive overload, where the brain struggles to process and retain information, resulting in frustration and discouragement. Instead, dissecting each subject into manageable segments allows for focused learning and gradual mastery. For example, if exploring machine learning, a learner might first understand its fundamental concepts before diving into specific algorithms like decision trees or support vector machines. Each small victory builds confidence and underscores an individual's capability to master more complex ideas over time.

Tailoring learning objectives to account for prior knowledge is also essential. Every learner embarks on their AI journey with different levels of understanding and expertise. Recognizing what one already knows enables the creation of personalized learning paths aligned with personal interests and career aspirations. Someone with a background in computer science might focus initially on deepening algorithmic understanding, while another individual with experience in data analysis might prioritize developing machine learning skills. By assessing and leveraging existing knowledge, goals become more relevant and attainable, making the learning experience more engaging and meaningful.

Creating a learning timeline is yet another critical component in structuring AI education. A timeline infuses discipline and routine into the learning process by assigning concrete deadlines to each objective. This method ensures a steady pace of progress while preventing procrastination—a common challenge when faced with long-term projects. An effective timeline incorporates short-term milestones alongside long-range goals, providing regular checkpoints to evaluate progress and adjust strategies as needed. For example, if the overarching aim is to complete a comprehensive AI certification program within a year, setting quarterly milestones to finish specific courses or projects helps maintain momentum and ensures that learners remain on track.

To illustrate, consider a professional aiming to enhance their skills to stay competitive in the workforce. By first identifying key areas of improvement, such as mastering a new AI tool or concept, they can set precise, time-bound objectives to achieve these skills within a targeted period. As they advance through their learning timeline, they can periodically assess their growing competencies against their broader career aspirations, adjusting their learning trajectory accordingly. This continuous feedback loop not only supports sustained growth but also boosts confidence, reinforcing the learner's commitment to their educational journey.

For educators incorporating AI into curricula, setting achievable learning objectives becomes even more impactful. They can design course modules that gradually increase in complexity, ensuring students develop a solid foundational understanding before progressing to more advanced topics. Educators can also encourage students to define their own SMART goals related to course content, fostering autonomy and motivating them to take ownership of their learning process. Such strategies not only help prevent overwhelm but also empower students to make meaningful connections between theoretical knowledge and practical application.

Connecting with AI Communities and Networks

Collaboration plays a vital role in enhancing our understanding and expanding opportunities within the field of artificial intelligence (AI). In an era where knowledge is constantly evolving, engaging with others who share similar interests can provide fresh insights and support. Online forums and discussion groups are particularly valuable for individuals at various stages of their AI learning journey. These platforms serve as a collective space where beginners can seek guidance from more experienced practitioners, professionals can collaborate on complex challenges, and educators can exchange teaching strategies. The diversity of participants leads to diverse perspectives, fostering an environment rich in innovative ideas and inspiring solutions.

To begin your journey in finding supportive online communities, it's beneficial to explore well-known forums such as Reddit's Machine Learning subreddit or AI-related groups on platforms like LinkedIn. These spaces not only offer the chance to pose questions and receive expert advice but also allow you to witness discussions on emerging AI trends and technologies. Participating actively by asking thoughtful questions or sharing your own knowledge can establish you as a valued member of these communities, opening doors to unexpected collaborations.

Moving from the digital sphere to face-to-face interactions, local meetups and workshops present unique opportunities to connect directly with peers, experts, and enthusiasts in your area. Unlike online interactions, these gatherings facilitate personal connections through conversations, networking events, and presentations. Attending a local AI meetup could mean the difference between working on your projects in isolation and partnering with someone whose skills complement yours. These events often feature talks by industry experts, offering firsthand insight into cutting-edge research, practical applications, and career development opportunities.

For those keen on participating in meetups, one effective approach is to explore platforms like Meetup.com, which host numerous AI-focused events. By joining, you gain access to a calendar of upcoming gatherings tailored to your interests. Keep an eye out for events that include workshops or hands-on sessions, as these can enhance your learning experience through practical engagement. These meetups are an excellent place to cultivate long-term relationships that might lead to exciting collaborative endeavors.

Another avenue to consider is becoming a member of professional organizations dedicated to AI and technology. These associations often provide an array of resources, including webinars, publications, and conferences, designed to keep members informed about industry developments. Being a part of such organizations grants access to exclusive events where you can network with leaders and pioneers in the field. These events are ideal platforms for showcasing your work and achievements, enabling you to gain visibility and credibility within the AI community.

Organizations like the Association for Computing Machinery (ACM) offer memberships that come with benefits such as subscriptions to academic journals and discounts on conference registrations. This involvement not only supplements your knowledge but also allows you to contribute to the field through presentation opportunities or collaborative research. Engaging with these organizations can help map your career path and position you strategically within the competitive landscape.

Lastly, leveraging social media to engage with AI thought leaders can significantly broaden your horizons. Platforms such as Twitter and LinkedIn have become instrumental in disseminating information at an unprecedented pace. By following key figures and organizations in AI, you can remain updated on the latest advancements, debates, and opportunities. What's more, social media can act as a bridge to mentorship. Many AI experts use these channels to share their insights and occasionally provide direct responses to followers' queries.

When utilizing social media effectively, curate your feed to include a mix of influencers, researchers, and companies driving innovation in AI. Engage actively by commenting thoughtfully on posts, sharing relevant content, or even reaching out via direct messages to build rapport. Personalized interactions can lead to informal mentorships with professionals willing to guide you along your journey.

Leveraging Online Courses and Certifications

Harnessing the power of online resources is an essential part of building a solid foundation in artificial intelligence (AI). With advancements in technology, reputable platforms now offer comprehensive courses that accommodate the busy schedules of learners. For those starting their AI journey or professionals sharpening their skills, these courses are designed with flexible pacing, ensuring you can balance learning with other commitments. The expertise of experienced instructors enhances your understanding, bringing clarity to complex topics and providing insights from real-world experiences. Furthermore, such courses often come with industry-recognized content, aligning educational materials with current market demands.

Online certifications play a vital role in substantiating one's proficiency in AI. Securing formal certifications not only verifies your knowledge but significantly boosts your employment prospects. Employers frequently seek candidates whose skills have been formally acknowledged, using certifications as a benchmark to gauge capabilities. This credential serves as a testament to your dedication and expertise, offering you a competitive edge in the fast-paced job market. By completing recognized certifications, you demonstrate to potential employers that you possess the requisite skills and commitment necessary for roles in this evolving field.

Emphasizing hands-on learning, project-based courses provide invaluable practical experience. These courses encourage learners to actively apply theoretical knowledge to real-world scenarios. By engaging in projects, you gain tangible outputs for your portfolio, showcasing your ability to tackle practical challenges. This experience deepens your understanding of AI concepts and operations, transcending beyond academic learning. The process of creating models, analyzing data, or designing algorithms offers insights into the intricacies of AI, enhancing problem-solving skills and fostering innovation.

Coursework integrated with projects often culminates in a diverse portfolio, which becomes a powerful tool when seeking opportunities within the industry. Employers value the demonstration of abilities through practical examples, appreciating a candidate's competence and readiness to contribute effectively. Actively participating in project-based learning prepares you for the dynamic expectations of AI roles, ensuring you can perform tasks efficiently and creatively.

Collaborative learning environments such as study groups add another dimension to your educational journey. Engaging in study groups fosters accountability, motivating you to maintain consistent study habits. Through shared responsibility, group members hold each other accountable, ensuring tasks and goals are met. These interactions aid knowledge retention, as discussing and debating different concepts solidify learning. Moreover, study groups simulate professional teamwork, preparing you for collaborative efforts in workplace settings where cooperation and effective communication are paramount.

Participation in study groups also cultivates a community of support and encouragement. When tackling challenging topics, having peers to consult and collaborate with can break down complex subjects into manageable parts. This communal learning approach reinforces understanding and builds confidence, equipping you with strategies to overcome difficult problems, both theoretically and practically.

In addition, being part of study communities encourages diversity of thought. Exposure to various perspectives enriches your learning experience, allowing you to appreciate different approaches to problem-solving. This diversity mirrors real-world working environments, where cross-disciplinary collaboration is crucial for innovative solutions. By actively engaging with peers, you develop skills not just in AI, but in leadership and empathy, qualities essential for professional growth and success.

As you navigate the landscape of AI education, consider combining these learning methods—online courses, certifications, project-based experiences, and collaborative study—to create a balanced and robust learning strategy. Each component addresses unique aspects of the educational experience, collectively supporting a comprehensive understanding of AI and its applications.

To maximize your learning outcomes, it's beneficial to strategically select courses and certifications that align with your career objectives. Researching course content, instructor credentials, and platform reputation ensures you invest your time in worthwhile educational pursuits. Seek programs that prioritize practical application alongside theoretical instruction, as this combination proves most effective in mastering AI competencies.

Remember, continuous learning is key in the ever-evolving sphere of AI. Staying updated with new technologies and methodologies will keep your skills relevant and valuable. Pursue additional training opportunities, attend workshops, and participate in webinars to expand your knowledge base and remain at the forefront of innovation.

Staying Updated with AI Trends and Innovations

In the ever-evolving world of artificial intelligence (AI), staying informed about the latest advancements is not just beneficial—it's essential. As the AI landscape shifts rapidly, maintaining a current understanding of developments ensures that you remain competitive and knowledgeable in this exciting field. One effective way to keep up with AI trends is through industry newsletters. These newsletters often provide curated content, bringing together expert opinions and analyses that offer insights into recent breakthroughs, regulatory changes, and emerging technologies. Subscribing to these resources means you receive regular updates right in your inbox, making it convenient to stay engaged with the AI community.

Another invaluable resource for continuous learning is social media. Following influential AI experts on platforms such as Twitter or LinkedIn can connect you directly with thought leaders who are shaping the future of AI. These individuals frequently share their perspectives on recent studies, technological innovations, and ethical considerations. By following them, you gain access to firsthand information and can engage in discussions that broaden your understanding. Social media offers a dynamic environment where you can participate in conversations, ask questions, and even contribute your own thoughts, thus becoming an active participant in the AI discourse.

Webinars and virtual conferences present further opportunities to expand your AI knowledge. These events bring together experts from various fields to discuss current trends, challenges, and innovations in AI. Attending webinars allows you to hear directly from leaders who are at the forefront of research and development. Moreover, these sessions often include interactive elements such as Q&A segments, enabling you to clarify doubts and gather insights that could be crucial for your personal or professional projects. Additionally, webinars create networking possibilities, allowing you to connect with like-minded individuals who share your passion for AI.

It is helpful here to follow a guideline when participating in webinars: assess the credentials of the speakers and the relevance of the topic to ensure that you're investing your time wisely. Make sure to prepare ahead of time by reviewing related materials, so you can engage more thoroughly during the session. Taking notes and reflecting on what you've learned afterward can also enhance retention and application of new knowledge.

Reading academic journals is another critical component of your AI learning journey. These publications delve into technical details, exploring theories and methodologies that underpin AI technologies. By regularly reading journals, you build a deeper understanding of complex concepts and develop critical thinking skills that help you analyze and apply AI principles effectively. Journals often serve as a bridge between theoretical study and practical application, ensuring that your projects align with current research standards. They challenge you to question assumptions, test hypotheses, and explore diverse approaches to problem-solving.

Engaging with academic literature also keeps you abreast of emerging research areas and potential future developments. This awareness can inspire innovation and guide your educational or career pursuits within AI.

Understanding the nuances of current research helps refine your skills, making you a more adaptable and informed practitioner or educator in the field.

For beginners, professionals, educators, and students alike, ongoing engagement with these resources is vital. Beginners benefit from gaining foundational knowledge and exposure to practical applications, while professionals enhance their expertise to stay competitive in the workforce. Educators can incorporate the latest AI concepts into their curricula, enriching their teaching and preparing their students for future roles in technology-driven environments. Students pursuing STEM careers can integrate AI insights with their existing studies, improving both their employability and interdisciplinary collaboration skills.

Integrating Learned Knowledge into Practice

The journey into AI can often seem daunting, particularly when trying to translate theoretical knowledge into practical applications. However, embracing hands-on projects and real-world scenarios is essential for solidifying understanding. These experiences go beyond the textbooks, offering learners the opportunity to apply algorithms in tangible settings, such as predicting stock market trends or developing recommendation systems for e-commerce platforms. These projects not only reinforce theoretical principles but also reveal practical challenges like data inadequacies and computational limitations that are inherent in AI development.

Collaborating on AI projects further enhances this learning process by opening doors to shared expertise and diverse perspectives. When individuals come together to tackle a problem, they bring unique skills and insights. For instance, a data scientist may focus on model building while a software engineer fine-tunes the implementation. This diversity leads to innovative approaches and robust solutions. Moreover, collaborative environments foster problem-solving skills essential in the professional world, where interdisciplinary teams are standard. It encourages learning from peers, adapting new techniques, and refining one's methodology based on collaborative feedback.

Reflective practice is another critical component of bridging this gap between theory and application. By reflecting on outcomes and being receptive to feedback, learners can pinpoint areas of improvement and adapt their strategies accordingly. This process involves analyzing what worked well in a project, identifying mistakes, and adjusting future actions. It's about asking questions like, "How could I have achieved better accuracy?" or "What other models might have been more effective?" Reflective practice not only promotes continual learning but also helps individuals become more adaptive in a field known for its rapid advancements.

Participation in hackathons and coding challenges offers a dynamic way to test skills and encourage creativity. These competitions simulate high-pressure environments often found in the tech industry, pushing participants to think quickly and creatively. Hackathons challenge individuals to develop fully functional prototypes within tight deadlines, often leading to unexpected innovations and creative problem-solving tactics. Moreover, these events provide a platform for showcasing capabilities, whether it's through winning prizes or simply gaining recognition among peers and potential employers. They also offer networking opportunities with industry professionals who may offer invaluable advice or even future career opportunities.

While engaging in these activities, it's crucial to set clear objectives and measure progress regularly. This structured approach ensures that learning remains focused and aligned with personal and professional goals. Additionally, seeking mentorship from experienced AI practitioners can provide guidance and deepen understanding, offering insights into overcoming common hurdles. Mentors can provide real-world examples of how they've bridged the theory-practice gap, highlighting strategies and mindsets that lead to success.

CONCLUSION

As we reach the end of our exploration into the world of artificial intelligence, it's time to reflect on the key concepts we've traversed and understand their significance. This journey was crafted to guide beginners, professionals seeking to enhance their technical acumen, educators eager to integrate AI into their curricula, and students aiming for a robust foundation in STEM fields. Each chapter has meticulously built on foundational knowledge, culminating in a comprehensive framework that not only elucidates the intricacies of AI but also empowers you to wield it effectively.

From the outset, we delved into the fundamental concepts that underpin artificial intelligence, setting the stage for understanding more complex subjects later on. By grasping these basics, you've unlocked the potential to explore advanced topics like neural networks and generative AI. This structured approach ensures that each segment of learning reinforces the next, crafting a cohesive narrative that demystifies AI's complexities. This alignment across topics offers you not just a cursory glance, but a profound insight into this transformative technology, enabling you to perceive how these components interconnect in real-world applications.

Yet, understanding theory without practical application limits its utility. Throughout this book, we emphasized the importance of translating conceptual knowledge into real-world skills. The exercises interspersed within the chapters aren't merely academic tasks—they serve as pivotal tools for embedding AI principles into your professional toolkit. Whether you're constructing a basic classification model, experimenting with neural networks, or designing your first chatbot, these hands-on activities are crucial. They transform theoretical frameworks into tangible skills, equipping you with the capability to innovate and solve challenges through AI.

The transformative potential of AI lies not only in understanding its principles but also in applying them creatively. Practical engagement solidifies understanding and sharpens competency, bridging the gap between abstract concepts and functional expertise. As such, each exercise was intentionally designed to foster incremental growth, pushing you to experiment, refine your techniques, and ultimately master the application of AI in diverse settings.

In the rapidly evolving landscape of technology, complacency is the enemy. The field of artificial intelligence is dynamic, characterized by continuous advancements that redefine what we know and can do. Thus, embracing a mindset of perpetual learning is paramount. Your journey shouldn't conclude with this book; instead, let it be a springboard into lifelong education. Stay curious and engaged with the ever-expanding horizons of AI by participating in online courses, joining spirited AI communities, and exploring cutting-edge research. These avenues will ensure that your skills remain sharp and your knowledge up-to-date, fostering adaptability in this fast-paced domain.

Adapting to the constant evolution of AI technology is not merely a professional necessity—it's an opportunity. The insights gained here equip you to pivot and respond to emerging trends, fortifying your position in your chosen field. By staying abreast of developments, you solidify your role as a proactive contributor who leverages AI's advancements rather than reacting passively to changes. Such preparedness positions you to integrate the latest innovations seamlessly, maintaining relevance and competitive advantage.

Ultimately, the culmination of knowledge and skill acquisition should inspire action. Now is the moment to envision where AI can elevate your career, studies, or teaching methodologies. Identify areas ripe for enhancement through AI's capabilities. Perhaps there's a process crying out for automation, a routine task begging for efficiency, or a project whose impact could be amplified via AI tools. The possibilities, boundless and invigorating, lie at your fingertips.

Embark on this path with confidence, taking concrete steps towards integrating AI into your work. Dare to experiment with new strategies and cultivate an environment of innovation. By embracing the tools and techniques discussed throughout this book, you harness the power of AI to drive meaningful change. You become an architect of transformation, reshaping workflows, educational paradigms, or scientific inquiries with precision and creativity.

Don't view the culmination of this reading journey as an endpoint but as the genesis of a new phase of exploration and implementation. Grounded in the fundamentals and equipped with practice, you're ready to embark on projects that showcase AI's ability to revolutionize industries and educational landscapes. Challenge traditional boundaries, foster interdisciplinary collaborations, and contribute meaningfully to the dialogue surrounding AI's ethical, societal, and technological implications.

As you apply your newfound knowledge, remember to share your journey with others. Collaboration enriches both personal growth and collective understanding. By engaging with peers, mentors, or students, you not only reinforce your own learning but also catalyze the ripple effect of knowledge dissemination. Inspire those around you to embark on similar journeys of discovery, creating a culture of curiosity and innovation that propels everyone forward.

As you close this book, take away a vision: see yourself as an active participant in the AI-driven future. In whatever field you inhabit, AI presents opportunities to challenge norms, push boundaries, and craft pioneering solutions. Embolden yourself to iterate upon existing systems, spearhead initiatives that weave AI into the fabric of everyday operations, and advocate for responsible, ethical AI development.

This conclusion is not merely a wrap-up of content but an invitation—a call to action. It beckons you to seize the momentum of your learning journey, courageously step into the realm of practical application, and continuously expand your horizon. Artificial Intelligence is not just a tool but a catalyst, one that will redefine careers, reshape industries, and reimagine education. Your role, whether as a learner, educator, or professional, is to channel its potential, creating value and driving progress. The future awaits your contribution; step confidently into it, armed with the knowledge and skills cultivated here.

As athank you for your interestand support, we are excited to offer an exclusive bonus to enhance yourreading experience. In addition to the main content, you now have access to a free downloadable bonus book.This additional resource is designed to further deepen your understanding and provide even more value to your journey.

Download Your Bonus Book To claim your free bonus book,simply scan the QR code below with your smartphone or tablet.

The download will start automatically after scanning

www.ingramcontent.com/pod-product-compliance
Lightning Source LLC
Chambersburg PA
CBHW070835070326
40690CB00009B/1553